George Putnam

**A Book of Common Worship**

George Putnam

**A Book of Common Worship**

ISBN/EAN: 9783337033866

Printed in Europe, USA, Canada, Australia, Japan

Cover: Foto ©Lupo / pixelio.de

More available books at **www.hansebooks.com**

# A BOOK OF COMMON WORSHIP

PREPARED UNDER DIRECTION OF THE NEW YORK STATE CONFERENCE OF RELIGION BY A COMMITTEE ON THE POSSIBILITIES OF COMMON WORSHIP

"Vox quidem dissona; sed una religio"
St. Ambrose

G. P. PUTNAM'S SONS
NEW YORK AND LONDON
The Knickerbocker Press
1900

COPYRIGHT, 1900
BY
G. P. PUTNAM'S SONS

The Knickerbocker Press, New York

There are several sorts of religion, not only in different parts of the island, but even in every town. . . . Yet the greater and wiser sort of them worship none of these, but adore one eternal, invisible, infinite, and incomprehensible Deity. . . . Those among them that have not received our religion, do not fright any from it, and use none ill that goes over to it. . . . He (Utopus) judged it not fit to determine anything rashly, and seemed to doubt whether those different forms of religion might not all come from God, who might inspire men in a different manner, and be pleased with this variety.

Though there are many different forms of religion among them, yet all these, how various soever, agree in the main point, which is the worshipping the Divine Essence; and therefore there is nothing to be seen or heard in their temples in which the several persuasions among them may not agree; for every sect performs those rites that are peculiar to it in their private houses, nor is there anything in the public worship that contradicts the particular ways of those different sects. . . . Nor are there any prayers among them but such as every one of them may use without prejudice to his own opinion. . . . Both priests and people offer up very solemn prayers to God in a set form of words; and these are so composed, that whatsoever is pronounced by the whole assembly may be likewise applied by every man in particular to his own condition.

*Utopia: Sir Thomas More.*

# Preface

THE New York State Conference of Religion is an outgrowth of the National Congress of Religion, which itself was the child of the Parliament of Religions held in connection with the World's Fair, in Chicago, in the year 1893.

The Parliament of Religions was the first gathering of its kind in the history of the world — an assemblage of representatives of the various religions on earth, meeting together for a free and frank statement of their thought; with the view of promoting, not only kindlier tolerance, but a juster understanding by each of the others' faiths, a mutual recognition of the common truths embodied in all their religions, and the awakening, thus, of the spirit of brotherliness among the children of the All-Father. The remarkable impression of that Parliament on those who attended it has been only equalled by the quiet influence which has followed it in the direction of such universality in religion.

The National Congress of Religion aims, in a quiet way, to carry on this work in our own land, by gathering together representatives of all religions found upon our shores, in annual sessions, in different parts of the country. Several such sessions have been held, with marked influences for good.

The New York State Conference of Religion, in full sympathy with this work, purposes to promote the harmonious co-operation of all religious men for the furtherance of those religious, moral, and social ends which are vital alike to Church and Commonwealth.

In preparing for this Conference, the Executive Committee appointed, in the spring of 1900, a Sub-Committee to consider the Possibilities of Common Worship. That Committee reported in May, urging the importance of the element of worship in such a conference, and suggesting certain scripture readings, and a few hymns, with the use of the prayer "Our Father" following upon silent prayer.

The consideration of this report by the Executive Committee determined the Sub-Committee to enlarge greatly the scope of its original plan ; to prepare more extensive scripture readings, both from the Old and

# Preface

the New Testaments and from the Ethnic Scriptures; to make a selection of collects, or short prayers, such as could be used unhesitatingly in such an assemblage; and to follow these with a goodly number of hymns suitable for such an occasion.

This little book is the outgrowth of that work of the Committee on the Possibilities of Common Worship.

It is published with the hope, not only that it may be found useful in the sessions of the Conference, but also that other State Conferences and similar gatherings may make use of it; that independent religious societies may perhaps find it helpful in the development of their worship; and that it may prove helpful spiritually to many individuals in their own private use.

It is believed that such a Book of Common Worship may prove in itself an object-lesson in the Possibilities of Common Worship.

The selections from the Jewish and Christian Scriptures have been made either from the King James or the Revised Version, as has seemed best in each case; the responsive readings from the Old Testament being taken from selections used in the Synagogue worship.

The readings from the Ethnic Scriptures have been taken from the edition of the Sacred Books of the East, issued under the general editorship of Prof. Max Müller; with the exception, of course, that selections from the works not contained therein have been taken from such standard editions as Jowett's *Plato* and Long's *Marcus Aurelius* and *Epictetus*. A few selections have been made from Conway's *Sacred Anthology* and Schermerhorn's *Sacred Scriptures of the World*.

The prayers have been selected from Jewish offices and from various early Christian liturgies, from the offices of the Eastern Church and of the Roman Church, from the Book of Common Prayer, and from various private books of devotion of modern times as well as of earlier periods. No further liberties have been taken with any of these prayers than was necessary for the purpose of this manual. For obvious reasons, the formula in latter times closing many Christian collects has been omitted. In this we return to the earlier usage. All omissions are duly indicated. In prayers written in the singular number, as by Thomas à Kempis and St. Augustine, and in one instance in the Jewish Liturgy, we have used the plural number.

# Preface

For the hymns chosen for this manual the freest range of selection has been taken.

The imperfections of this little manual may perhaps be excused by reason of the haste necessary in preparing it for a special need. None will be more sensible of them than its compilers. It will have served its end if it prompt to a similar work undertaken in ampler leisure.

*Committee on the Possibilities of Common Worship.* { R. HEBER NEWTON, GUSTAV GOTTHEIL, THOMAS R. SLICER.

# Contents

I. SCRIPTURE READINGS.                                      PAGE

   A. Jewish and Christian Scriptures.              1
      a. Universality in Religion  .          1
      b. Ethical and Spiritual Religion  .   15
      c. Religion in Society and the State .  49
      d. Responsive Readings   .             67

   B. Ethnic Scriptures [Hindu, Persian, Chinese, Egyptian, Buddhist, Grecian, Roman, and Mohammedan].   79
      a. Universality in Religion  .         79
      b. Ethical and Spiritual Religion      91
      c. Religion in Society and the State . 197

II. PRAYERS.

   A. Collects of Universality   .   .          213
   B. Collects of Ethical and Spiritual Religion  .  .  .  .  .  .  251
   C. Collects of Religion—Society and the State  .  .  .  .  .  . 291
   D. Doxologies and Benedictions  .   301

III. HYMNS.

    A. Hymns of Universality . . . . 305
    B. Hymns of Natural, Ethical, and Spiritual Religion. . . . . . 325
    C. Hymns of Religion—Society and the State . . . . . . 381

IV. INDEX: Sources, Authors, Dates, etc. .

# I

# Scripture Readings

## A. Jewish and Christian Scriptures

### a. Universality in Religion

# I

# Scripture Readings

## A. Jewish and Christian Scriptures

### a. Universality in Religion

I. And God created man in His own image, in the image of God created He him; male and female created He them.

And Pharaoh said unto his servants, Can we find such a one as this Joseph (the Hebrew), a man in whom the spirit of God is?

Thou shalt not abhor an Edomite; for he is thy brother: thou shalt not abhor an Egyptian; because thou wast a stranger in his land.

Thus saith the Lord to His anointed, to Cyrus (the Persian), whose right hand I have holden, to subdue nations before him, and I will loose the loins of kings; to open the doors before him, and the gates shall not be shut; I will go before thee, and make the rugged places plain; I will break in pieces the doors of brass, and cut in sunder the bars of iron; and I will give thee the treasures of darkness, and hidden riches of secret places, that thou mayest know that I am the Lord, which call thee by thy name, even the God of Israel.

The Lord is in His holy temple; let all the earth keep silence before Him.

From the rising of the sun even unto the going down of the same my name is great among the Gentiles; and in every place incense is offered unto my name, and a pure offering: for my name is great among the Gentiles, saith the Lord of hosts.

II. Ben Zoma was in the habit of saying: Who is a wise man? He who learns from everybody; for thus it is written: From all who could teach me, I have sought to learn. Who is a hero? He who conquers his passions;

thus the Scriptures say: He that is slow to anger is better than the mighty, and he that ruleth his spirit than he that taketh a city. Who is a rich man? He who is satisfied with his lot; for thus it is said: When thou shalt eat the labor of thy hands; happy shalt thou be and it shall be well with thee. Happy shalt thou be in this world; it shall be well with thee in the world to come. Who is honored? He who honors his fellowmen; for thus it is written: Them that honor me I will honor, and they that despise me shall be lightly esteemed.

Ben Azzai was in the habit of saying: Be zealous in the practice of the slightest virtue, and flee from all manner of sin; for one virtue brings another in its wake, and one sin entails another; for the reward of virtue is virtue itself, and sin is requited with sin. He likewise said: Despise no man, and consider nothing as too far removed to come to pass, for there is no man but hath his day, and nothing but hath its place.

Rabbi Simeon was wont to say: There are three crowns: the crown of the Law, the crown of the priesthood, and the crown of royalty. But the crown of a fair name excelleth them all.

Rabbi Jacob said: This world is, as it were, the antechamber of the world hereafter; prepare thyself in the antechamber that thou mayest be admitted to the banqueting hall.

Rabbi Elazar Hakkapar said: Those born into the world are doomed to die; the dead, but to live on again, and those who enter the eternal life, to be judged. Therefore, let it be recognized, understood, and remembered, that He, the Almighty, the Creator, the Architect, He is the counsellor; He the judge; He the witness; He the accuser. He is always ready to give judgment: and before Him there is no injustice, no oversight, no regard for rank, no bribery. Know that all will appear in the account. Accept not the assurance of thy passions that the grave will be a place of refuge for thee. For without thy consent wert thou created, wert thou born into the world without thy choice; thou art now living without thine own volition, without thine approval thou wilt have to die; so likewise, without thy consent thou wilt have to render account between the Supreme King, the Holy One, blessed be He!

III. And one of them, a lawyer, asked him a question, tempting him, Master, which is the great commandment in the Law? And he said unto him, Thou shalt love the Lord thy God with all thy heart, and with all thy soul, and with all thy mind. This is the great and first commandment. And a second like unto it is this, Thou shalt love thy neighbor as thyself. On these two commandments hangeth the whole Law, and the Prophets.

And they shall come from the east and west, and from the north and south, and shall sit down in the kingdom of God.

The woman saith unto him, . . . Our fathers worshipped in this mountain; and ye say, that in Jerusalem is the place where men ought to worship. Jesus saith unto her, Woman, believe me, the hour cometh, when neither in this mountain, nor in Jerusalem, shall ye worship the Father. . . . But the hour cometh, and now is, when the true worshippers shall worship the Father in spirit and truth: for such doth the Father seek to be His worshippers. God is a Spirit: and they that worship Him must worship in spirit and truth.

And other sheep I have, which are not of this fold: them also I must bring, and they shall hear my voice; and they shall become one flock, one shepherd.

IV. And he came to Nazareth, where he had been brought up: and he entered, as his custom was, into the synagogue on the sabbath day, and stood up to read. And there was delivered unto him the book of the prophet Isaiah. And he opened the book, and found the place where it was written :

The Spirit of the Lord is upon me,
Because he anointed me to preach good tidings to the poor:
He hath sent me to proclaim release to the captives,
And recovering of sight to the blind,
To set at liberty them that are bruised,
To proclaim the acceptable year of the Lord.

And he closed the book, and gave it back to the attendant, and sat down: and the eyes of all in the synagogue were fastened on him. And he began to say unto them, To-day hath this scripture been fulfilled in your ears. And all bare him witness, and wondered at

the words of grace which proceeded out of
his mouth: and they said, Is not this Joseph's
son? And he said unto them. Doubtless ye
will say unto me this parable, Physician, heal
thyself: whatsoever we have heard done at
Capernaum, do also here in thine own
country. And he said, Verily I say unto
you, No prophet is acceptable in his own
country. But of a truth I say unto you,
There were many widows in Israel in the
days of Elijah, when the heaven was shut up
three years and six months, when there came
a great famine over all the land; and unto
none of them was Elijah sent, but only to
Zarephath, in the land of Sidon, unto a
woman that was a widow. And there were
many lepers in Israel in the time of Elisha
the prophet; and none of them was cleansed,
but only Naaman the Syrian.

V. And when the day of Pentecost was
fully come, they were all with one accord in
one place. And suddenly there came a
sound from heaven as of a rushing mighty
wind, and it filled all the house where they
were sitting. And there appeared unto them
cloven tongues like as of fire, and it sat upon
each of them. And they were all filled with

the Holy Ghost, and began to speak with other tongues as the Spirit gave them utterance. And there were dwelling at Jerusalem Jews, devout men, out of every nation under heaven. Now when this was noised abroad, the multitude came together, and were confounded, because that every man heard them speak in his own language. And they were all amazed and marvelled, saying one to another, Behold, are not all these which speak Galileans? And how hear we every man in our own tongue, wherein we were born? Parthians and Medes, and Elamites, and the dwellers in Mesopotamia, and in Judea, and Cappadocia, in Pontus, and Asia, Phrygia and Pamphylia, in Egypt, and in the parts of Libya about Cyrene, and strangers of Rome, Jews and proselytes, Cretes and Arabians, we do hear them speak in our tongues the wonderful works of God.

VI. There was a man sent from God, whose name was John. The same came for a witness, to bear witness of the Light, that all men through him might believe. He was not that Light, but was sent to bear witness of that Light. The true Light, which lighteth every man, was coming on into the world.

He was in the world, and the world was made through him, and the world knew him not. He came into his own possessions, and his own people received him not. But as many as received him, to them gave he power to become the sons of God, even to them that believe on his name: which were born, not of blood, nor of the will of the flesh, nor of the will of man, but of God.

VII. And Paul stood in the midst of the Areopagus, and said:

Ye men of Athens, in all things I perceive that ye are very religious. For as I passed along, and observed the objects of your worship, I found also an altar with this inscription, TO AN UNKNOWN GOD. What therefore ye worship in ignorance, this set I forth unto you. God that made the world and all things therein, seeing that He is Lord of heaven and earth, dwelleth not in temples made with hands: neither is He served by men's hands, as though He needed any thing, seeing He Himself giveth to all life, and breath, and all things; and He hath made of one blood all nations of men for to dwell on all the face of the earth, having determined their appointed seasons, and the bounds of their habitation;

that they should seek God, if haply they might feel after Him, and find Him, though He be not far from each one of us: for in Him we live, and move, and have our being; as certain even of your own poets have said, For we are also His offspring.

VIII. Who will render to every man according to his deeds: To them who by patient continuance in well doing seek for glory and honor and immortality, eternal life: But unto them that are contentious, and do not obey the truth, but obey unrighteousness, indignation, and wrath, tribulation and anguish, upon every soul of man that doeth evil, of the Jew first, and also of the Gentile; but glory, honor, and peace to every man that worketh good, to the Jew first, and also to the Gentile: For there is no respect of persons with God.

Is He the God of the Jews only? Is He not also of the Gentiles? Yes, of the Gentiles also.

For as many as are led by the Spirit of God, they are the sons of God.

For there is no distinction between Jew and Greek: for the same Lord is Lord of all, and is rich unto all that call upon Him: for, Whosoever shall call upon the name of the Lord shall be saved.

I therefore, the prisoner of the Lord, beseech you that ye walk worthy of the vocation wherewith ye are called, with all lowliness and meekness, with long suffering, forbearing one another in love; endeavoring to keep the unity of the Spirit in the bond of peace.

*b. Ethical and Spiritual Religion*

## b. Ethical and Spiritual Religion

IX. Hear, O Israel: the Lord our God is one Lord: and thou shalt love the Lord thy God with all thine heart, and with all thy soul, and with all thy might.

For this commandment which I command thee this day, it is not too hard for thee, neither is it far off. It is not in heaven, that thou shouldest say, Who shall go up for us to heaven, and bring it unto us, and make us to hear it, that we may do it? Neither is it beyond the sea, that thou shouldest say, Who shall go over the sea for us, and bring it unto us, and make us to hear it, that we may do it? But the word is very nigh unto thee, in thy mouth, and in thy heart, that thou mayest do it.

X.
Now a thing was secretly brought to me,
And mine ear received a whisper thereof.

In thoughts from the visions of the night,
When deep sleep falleth on men,
Fear came upon me, and trembling,
Which made all my bones to shake.
Then a spirit passed before my face;
The hair of my flesh stood up.
It stood still, but I could not discern the appearance thereof;
A form was before mine eyes:
There was silence, and I heard a voice, saying,
Shall mortal man be more just than God?
Shall a man be more pure than his Maker?
Behold, He putteth no trust in his servants;
And his angels He chargeth with folly:
How much more them that dwell in houses of clay,
Whose foundation is in the dust,
Which are crushed before the moth!
Betwixt morning and evening they are destroyed:
They perish forever without any regarding it.
Is not their tent-cord plucked up within them?
They die, and that without wisdom.

XI.

But where shall wisdom be found?
And where is the place of understanding?

Man knoweth not the price thereof;
Neither is it found in the land of the living.
The deep saith, It is not in me:
And the sea saith, It is not with me.
It cannot be gotten for gold.
Neither shall silver be weighed for the price
    thereof.
It cannot be valued with the gold of Ophir,
With the precious onyx, or the sapphire.
Gold and glass cannot equal it.
Neither shall the exchange thereof be jewels
    of fine gold.
No mention shall be made of coral or of
    crystal:
Yea, the price of wisdom is above rubies.
The topaz of Ethiopia shall not equal it,
Neither shall it be valued with pure gold.
Whence then cometh wisdom?
And where is the place of understanding?
Seeing it is hid from the eyes of all living,
And kept close from the fowls of the air.
Destruction and Death say,
We have heard a rumor thereof with our ears.
God understandeth the way thereof,
And He knoweth the place thereof.
For He looketh to the ends of the earth,
And seeth under the whole heaven;
To make a weight for the wind;

Yea, He meteth out the waters by measure.
When He made a decree for the rain,
And a way for the lightning of the thunder:
Then did He see it, and declare it;
He established it, yea, and searched it out.
And unto man He said,
Behold, the fear of the Lord, that is wisdom;
And to depart from evil is understanding.

## XII.

For when the ear heard me, then it blessed me;
And when the eye saw me, it gave witness unto me:
Because I delivered the poor that cried,
The fatherless also, that had none to help him.
The blessing of him that was ready to perish came upon me:
And I caused the widow's heart to sing for joy.
I put on righteousness, and it clothed me:
My justice was as a robe and a diadem.
I was eyes to the blind,
And feet was I to the lame.
I was a father to the needy:
And the cause of him that I knew not I searched out.

And I brake the jaws of the unrighteous,
And plucked the prey out of his teeth.

### XIII.

If I did despise the cause of my manservant
    or of my maidservant,
When they contended with me:
What then shall I do when God riseth up?
And when He visiteth, what shall I answer
    Him?
Did not He that made me in the womb make
    him?
And did not one fashion us in the womb?
If I have withheld the poor from their desire,
Or have caused the eyes of the widow to fail;
Or have eaten my morsel alone,
And the fatherless hath not eaten thereof;
(Nay, from my youth he grew up with me as
    with a father,
And I have been her guide from my mother's
    womb;)
If I have seen any perish for want of clothing,
Or that the needy had no covering;
If his loins have not blessed me,
And if he were not warmed with the fleece of
    my sheep;
If I have lifted up my hand against the
    fatherless,

Because I saw my help in the gate;
Then let my shoulder fall from the shoulder
 blade,
And mine arm be broken from the bone.

. . . . .

If I have made gold my hope,
And have said to the fine gold, Thou art my
 confidence;
If I rejoiced because my wealth was great,
And because mine hand had gotten much;

. . . . .

This also were an iniquity to be punished by
 the judges;
For I should have lied to God that is above.
If I rejoiced at the destruction of him that
 hated me,
Or lifted up myself when evil found him;

. . . . .

If the men of my tent said not,
Who can find one that hath not been satisfied
 with his flesh?
If like Adam I covered my transgressions,
By hiding mine iniquity in my bosom;
Because I feared the great multitude,
And the contempt of families terrified me,
So that I kept silence, and went not out of
 the door—

. . . . .

Surely I would carry it upon my shoulder;
I would bind it under me as a crown.
I would declare unto him the number of my steps;
As a prince would I go near unto him.
If my land cry out against me,
And the furrows thereof weep together;
If I have eaten the fruits thereof without money,
Or have caused the owners thereof to lose their life:
Let thistles grow instead of wheat,
And cockle instead of barley.

## XIV.

Lord, who shall sojourn in Thy tabernacle?
Who shall dwell in Thy holy hill?
He that walketh uprightly, and worketh righteousness,
And speaketh truth in his heart.
He that slandereth not with his tongue,
Nor doeth evil to his friend,
Nor taketh up a reproach against his neighbor.
In whose eyes a reprobate is despised;
But he honoreth them that fear the Lord.
He that sweareth to his own hurt, and changeth not.

He that putteth not out his money to usury,
Nor taketh reward against the innocent,
He that doeth these things shall never be moved.

XV.

The heavens declare the glory of God;
And the firmament sheweth His handiwork.
Day unto day uttereth speech,
And night unto night sheweth knowledge.
There is no speech nor language;
Their voice cannot be heard.
Their line is gone out through all the earth,
And their words to the end of the world.
In them hath He set a tabernacle for the sun,
Which is as a bridegroom coming out of his chamber,
And rejoiceth as a strong man to run his course.
His going forth is from the end of the heaven,
And his circuit unto the ends of it:
And there is nothing hid from the heat thereof.

The law of the Lord is perfect, restoring the soul:
The testimony of the Lord is sure, making wise the simple.

The precepts of the Lord are right, rejoicing the heart:
The commandment of the Lord is pure, enlightening the eyes.
The fear of the Lord is clean, enduring forever:
The judgments of the Lord are true, and righteous altogether.
More to be desired are they than gold, yea, than much fine gold:
Sweeter also than honey and the honeycomb.
Moreover by them is thy servant warned:
In keeping of them there is great reward.
Who can discern his errors?
Clear Thou me from hidden faults.
Keep back Thy servant also from presumptuous sins;
Let them not have dominion over me: then shall I be perfect,
And I shall be clear from great transgression.
Let the words of my mouth, and the meditation of my heart be acceptable in thy sight,
O Lord, my rock, and my redeemer.

XVI.

The Lord is my shepherd; I shall not want.
He maketh me to lie down in green pastures:

He leadeth me beside the still waters.
He restoreth my soul:
He guideth me in the paths of righteousness for His name's sake.
Yea, though I walk through the valley of the shadow of death,
I will fear no evil; for Thou art with me:
Thy rod and Thy staff, they comfort me.
Thou preparest a table before me in the presence of mine enemies:
Thou hast anointed my head with oil; my cup runneth over.
Surely goodness and mercy shall follow me all the days of my life:
And I will dwell in the house of the Lord forever.

XVII.

He that dwelleth in the secret place of the Most High
Shall abide under the shadow of the Almighty.
I will say of the Lord, He is my refuge and my fortress;
My God, in whom I trust.
For He shall deliver thee from the snare of the fowler,
And from the noisome pestilence.
He shall cover thee with His pinions,

And under His wings shalt thou take refuge:
His truth is a shield and a buckler.
Thou shalt not be afraid for the terror by night,
Nor for the arrow that flieth by day;
For the pestilence that walketh in darkness,
Nor for the destruction that wasteth at noonday.
A thousand shall fall at thy side,
And ten thousand at thy right hand;
But it shall not come nigh thee.
Only with thine eyes shalt thou behold,
And see the reward of the wicked.
For thou, O Lord, art my refuge!
Thou hast made the Most High thy habitation;
There shall no evil befall thee,
Neither shall any plague come nigh thy tent.
For He shall give His angels charge over thee,
To keep thee in all thy ways.
They shall bear thee up in their hands,
Lest thou dash thy foot against a stone.
Thou shalt tread upon the lion and adder:
The young lion and the serpent shalt thou trample under feet.
Because he hath set his love upon Me, therefore will I deliver him.
I will set him on high, because he hath known My name.

He shall call upon Me, and I will answer him;
I will be with him in trouble:
I will deliver him, and honor him.
With long life will I satisfy him,
And shew him My salvation.

### XVIII.

Bless the LORD, O my soul;
And all that is within me, bless His holy
    name.
Bless the LORD, O my soul,
And forget not all His benefits:
Who forgiveth all thine iniquities;
Who healeth all thy diseases;
Who redeemeth thy life from destruction;
Who crowneth thee with loving kindness and
    tender mercies:
Who satisfieth thy mouth with good things;
So that thy youth is renewed like the eagle.
The LORD executeth righteous acts,
And judgments for all that are oppressed.
He made known his ways unto Moses,
His doings unto the children of Israel.
The LORD is full of compassion and gracious,
Slow to anger, and plenteous in mercy.
He will not always chide;
Neither will He keep His anger forever.
He hath not dealt with us after our sins,

Nor rewarded us after our iniquities.
For as the heaven is high above the earth,
So great is His mercy toward them that fear Him.
As far as the east is from the west,
So far hath He removed our transgressions from us.
Like as a father pitieth his children,
So the LORD pitieth them that fear Him.
For He knoweth our frame;
He remembereth that we are dust.
As for man, his days are as grass;
As a flower of the field, so he flourisheth.
For the wind passeth over it, and it is gone;
And the place thereof shall know it no more.
But the mercy of the LORD is from everlasting to everlasting upon them that fear Him,
And his righteousness unto children's children:
To such as keep His covenant,
And to those that remember His precepts to do them.
The LORD hath established His throne in the heavens:
And His kingdom ruleth over all.
Bless the LORD, ye angels of His:
Ye mighty in strength, that fulfil His word,
Hearkening unto the voice of His word.

Bless the LORD, all ye His hosts;
Ye ministers of His, that do His pleasure.
Bless the LORD, all ye His works,
In all places of His dominion:
Bless the LORD, O my soul.

XIX.
Trust in the LORD with all thine heart,
And lean not upon thine own understanding:
In all thy ways acknowledge Him,
And He shall direct thy paths.
Be not wise in thine own eyes:
Fear the LORD, and depart from evil:
It shall be health to thy navel,
And marrow to thy bones.
Honor the LORD with thy substance,
And with the first fruits of all thine increase:
So shall thy barns be filled with plenty,
And thy vats shall overflow with new wine.

My son, despise not the chastening of the
    LORD:
Neither be weary of His reproof:
For whom the LORD loveth He reproveth;
Even as a father the son in whom he de-
    lighteth.
Happy is the man that findeth wisdom,
And the man that getteth understanding.

For the merchandise of it is better than the
 merchandise of silver,
And the gain thereof than fine gold.
She is more precious than rubies:
And none of the things thou canst desire are
 to be compared unto her.
Length of days is in her right hand:
In her left hand are riches and honor.
Her ways are ways of pleasantness,
And all her paths are peace.
She is a tree of life to them that lay hold
 upon her:
And happy is every one that retaineth her.
The LORD by wisdom founded the earth;
By understanding He established the heavens.
By His knowledge the depths were broken up,
And the skies drop down the dew.

### XX.

I wisdom have made subtilty my dwelling,
And find out knowledge and discretion.
The fear of the LORD is to hate evil:
Pride, and arrogancy, and the evil way,
And the froward mouth, do I hate.
Counsel is mine, and sound knowledge:
I am understanding; I have might.
By me kings reign,
And princes decree justice.

By me princes rule,
And nobles, even all the judges of the earth.
I love them that love me;
And those that seek me diligently shall find me.
Riches and honor are with me;
Yea, durable riches and righteousness.
My fruit is better than gold, yea, than fine gold;
And my revenue than choice silver.
I walk in the way of righteousness,
In the midst of the paths of judgment:
That I may cause those that love me to inherit substance,
And that I may fill their treasuries.
The LORD possessed me in the beginning of His way,
Before His works of old.
I was set up from everlasting, from the beginning,
Or ever the earth was.
When there were no depths, I was brought forth;
When there were no fountains abounding with water.
Before the mountains were settled,
Before the hills was I brought forth:

While as yet He had not made the earth, nor
    the fields,
Nor the beginning of the dust of the world.
When He established the heavens, I was
    there:
When He set a circle upon the face of the
    deep:
When He made firm the skies above:
When the fountains of the deep became
    strong:
When He gave to the sea its bound,
That the waters should not transgress His
    commandment:
When He marked out the foundations of the
    earth:
Then I was by Him, as a master workman:
And I was daily His delight,
Rejoicing always before Him;
Rejoicing in His habitable earth;
And my delight was with the sons of men.
Now therefore, my sons, hearken unto me:
For blessed are they that keep my ways.
Hear instruction, and be wise,
And refuse it not.
Blessed is the man that heareth me,
Watching daily at my gates,
Waiting at the posts of my doors.
For whoso findeth me findeth life,

And shall obtain favor of the Lord.
But he that sinneth against me wrongeth his
    own soul:
All they that hate me love death.

XXI. Comfort ye, comfort ye My people, saith your God. Speak ye comfortably to Jerusalem, and cry unto her, that her warfare is accomplished, that her iniquity is pardoned; that she hath received of the Lord's hand double for all her sins.

The voice of one that crieth, Prepare ye in the wilderness the way of the Lord, make straight in the desert a highway for our God. Every valley shall be exalted, and every mountain and hill shall be made low: and the crooked shall be made straight, and the rough places plain: and the glory of the Lord shall be revealed, and all flesh shall see it together: for the mouth of the Lord hath spoken it. The voice of one saying, Cry. And one said, What shall I cry? All flesh is grass, and all the goodliness thereof is as the flower of the field: the grass withereth, the flower fadeth; because the breath of the Lord bloweth upon it: surely the people is grass. The grass withereth, the flower fadeth: but the word of our God shall stand forever.

O thou that tellest good tidings to Zion, get thee up into the high mountain; O thou that tellest good tidings to Jerusalem, lift up thy voice with strength; lift it up, be not afraid; say unto the cities of Judah, Behold your God! Behold, the Lord God will come as a mighty one, and His arm shall rule for Him: behold, His reward is with Him, and His recompense before Him. He shall feed His flock like a shepherd, He shall gather the lambs in His arm, and carry them into His bosom, and shall gently lead those that give suck.

Who hath measured the waters in the hollow of His hand, and meted out heaven with the span, and comprehended the dust of the earth in a measure, and weighed the mountains in scales, and the hills in a balance? Who hath directed the spirit of the Lord, or being His counsellor hath taught Him? With whom took He counsel, and who instructed Him, and taught Him in the path of judgment, and taught Him knowledge, and shewed to Him the way of understanding? Behold, the nations are as a drop of a bucket, and are counted as the small dust of the balance: behold, He taketh up the isles as a very little thing. And Lebanon is not sufficient to burn, nor the beasts thereof sufficient for a burnt offering. All the nations are as nothing before Him; they are counted to Him less than nothing, and vanity. . . . To whom then will ye liken Me, that I should be equal to him? saith the Holy One. Lift up your eyes on high, and see who hath created these, that bringeth out their host by number: He calleth them all by name; by the greatness of His might, and for that He is strong in power, not one is lacking.

Why sayest thou, O Jacob, and speakest, O Israel, My way is hid from the Lord, and my judgment is passed away from my God? Hast thou not known? hast thou not heard? the everlasting God, the LORD, the Creator of the ends of the earth, fainteth not, neither is weary; there is no searching of His understanding. He giveth power to the faint; and to Him that hath no might He increaseth strength. Even the youths shall faint and be weary, and the young men shall utterly fall: but they that wait upon the Lord shall renew their strength; they shall mount up with wings as eagles; they shall run, and not be weary; they shall walk, and not faint.

XXII. Behold, the days come, saith the

Lord, that I will make a new covenant with the house of Israel, and with the house of Judah: not according to the covenant that I made with their fathers in the day that I took them by the hand to bring them out of the land of Egypt; which My covenant they brake, although I was an husband unto them, saith the Lord. But this is the covenant that I will make with the house of Israel after those days, saith the Lord; I will put My law in their inward parts, and in their heart will I write it; and I will be their God, and they shall be My people: and they shall teach no more every man his neighbor, and every man his brother, saying, Know the Lord: for they shall all know Me, from the least of them unto the greatest of them, saith the Lord: for I will forgive their iniquity, and their sin will I remember no more.

XXIII. Hear ye now what the Lord saith; Arise, contend thou before the mountains, and let the hills hear thy voice. Hear ye, O mountains, the Lord's controversy, and ye strong foundations of the earth: for the Lord hath a controversy with His people, and He will plead with Israel.

O my people, what have I done unto thee?

and wherein have I wearied thee? testify against Me. For I brought thee up out of the land of Egypt, and redeemed thee out of the house of servants; and I sent before thee Moses, Aaron and Miriam. O my people, remember now what Balak king of Moab consulted, and what Balaam the son of Beor answered him from Shittim unto Gilgal; that ye may know the righteousness of the Lord.

Wherewith shall I come before the Lord, and bow myself before the high God? Shall I come before him with burnt offerings, with calves of a year old? Will the Lord be pleased with thousands of rams, or with ten thousands of rivers of oil? Shall I give my firstborn for my transgression, the fruit of my body for the sin of my soul? He hath shewed thee, O man, what is good; and what doth the Lord require of thee, but to do justly, and to love mercy, and to walk humbly with thy God?

XXIV. The motto of Simon the Just was: The order of the world rests upon three things: on law, on worship, and on charity.

Antigonos of Sokho was in the habit of saying: Be not like servants who serve their master for the sake of the compensation; be like those who serve their master without a thought of reward.

Joshua ben Pera'hya said: Get thee a teacher, win a comrade, and judge every man from his favorable side.

Hillel said: Be a disciple of Aaron, love peace, pursue peace; love all men; and bring them nigh unto the Law.

Rabban Simeon ben Gamaliel was wont to say: All the days of my life have been passed among sages, and I have never found anything better for man than silence. Not research, but practice is of the most importance. He who talks much, cannot avoid sin.

He also said: Three things support the world, truth, justice, and peace: as the Scripture hints, "Execute the judgment of truth and peace in your gates."

XXV. Rabbi Judah was in the habit of saying: In choosing the right path, see that it is one which is honorable to thyself and without offence to others. Be as scrupulous about the lightest command as about the weightiest, for no man knoweth the result of his actions. Weigh the present temporal disadvantages of a dutiful course against the reward of the future, and the present desirable fruits of a sinful deed against the injury to thine immortal soul. In general, consider three things and thou wilt never fall into sin: remember that there is above thee an all-seeing eye, an all-hearing ear, and a record of all thy actions.

Hillel was in the habit of saying: Do not isolate thyself from the congregation and its interests. Do not rely upon thy spiritual strength until the day of thy death. Pass not judgment upon thy neighbor until thou hast put thyself in his place. Never say, Sometime or other, when I enjoy leisure, I will attend to my spiritual advancement; perhaps thou wilt never have the leisure.

He furthermore said: The more feasting, the more food for worms; the more wealth, the more cares. But the more knowledge, the more food for life; the more study, the more wisdom; the more reflection, the better the counsel; the more charity, the more peace. He who earns a good name gains something that can never be taken away.

Rabbi Jo'hanan ben Zakkai had the following five disciples: Rabbi Eliezer ben Hyrkan, Rabbi Joshua ben 'Hananyah, Rabbi Josè the Priest, Rabbi Simeon ben Nathaniel, and Rabbi Elazar ben Arakh. Once he said to them: Go forth and find out what is the best thing to cultivate. R. Eliezer said: A generous eye. R. Joshua said: A loyal friend. R. Josè said: A good neighbor. R. Simeon said: Prudence and foresight. R. Elazar said: A good heart. Thereupon R. Jo'hanan said: I consider R. Elazar ben Arakh's judgment the best, for in his answer all of yours are included.

Rabbi Josè used to say: Thy neighbor's property must be as sacred to thee as thine own. Let noble purpose underlie thine every action.

Rabbi Simeon used to say: Be particular in performing thy devotions at the proper time. Do not look upon prayer as a meaningless, obligatory task, but as a voluntary offering to God's mercy and grace. Neither think thyself too great a sinner to approach Him.

Rabbi Tarphon was in the habit of saying:

The day is short, the work is great, the workmen are slothful, the reward is rich, and the Master is urgent. He also said: It is not incumbent on thee to complete the whole task, but thou art not at liberty therefore to neglect it entirely.

XXVI. And seeing the multitudes, he went up into a mountain: and when he was set, his disciples came unto him: and he opened his mouth, and taught them, saying:

Blessed are the poor in spirit: for their's is the kingdom of heaven. Blessed are they that mourn: for they shall be comforted. Blessed are the meek: for they shall inherit the earth. Blessed are they which do hunger and thirst after righteousness: for they shall be filled. Blessed are the merciful: for they shall obtain mercy. Blessed are the pure in heart: for they shall see God. Blessed are the peacemakers: for they shall be called the children of God. Blessed are they which shall be persecuted for righteousness' sake: for their's is the kingdom of heaven. Blessed are ye, when men shall revile you, and persecute you, and shall say all manner of evil against you falsely, for my sake. Rejoice, and be exceeding glad: for great is your reward in heaven: for so persecuted they the prophets which were before you.

XXVII. Lay not up for yourselves treasures upon the earth, where moth and rust doth consume, and where thieves break through and steal: but lay up for yourselves treasures in heaven, where neither moth nor rust doth consume, and where thieves do not break through nor steal: for where thy treasure is, there will thy heart be also. The lamp of the body is the eye; if therefore thine eye be single, thy whole body shall be full of light. But if thine eye be evil, thy whole body shall be full of darkness. If therefore the light that is in thee be darkness, how great is the darkness! No man can serve two masters: for either he will hate the one, and love the other; or else he will hold to one, and despise the other. Ye cannot serve God and mammon. Therefore I say unto you, Be not anxious for your life, what ye shall eat, or what ye shall drink; nor yet for your body, what ye shall put on. Is not the life more than the food, and the body than the raiment? Behold the birds of heaven, that they sow not, neither do they reap, nor gather into barns; and your heavenly Father feedeth them. Are not ye of much more value than they? And which of you by being anxious can add one cubit unto his stature? And why are ye anxious concerning raiment? Consider the lilies of the field, how they grow; they toil not, neither do they spin: yet I say unto you, that even Solomon in all his glory was not arrayed like one of these. But if God doth so clothe the grass of the field, which to-day is, and to-morrow is cast into the oven, shall He not much more clothe you, O ye of little faith? Be not therefore anxious, saying, What shall we eat? or, What shall we drink? or, Wherewithal shall we be clothed? For after all these things do the Gentiles seek; for your heavenly Father knoweth that ye have need of all these things. But seek ye first His kingdom, and His righteousness; and all these things shall be added unto you. Be not therefore anxious for the morrow: for the morrow will be anxious for itself. Sufficient unto the day is the evil thereof.

XXVIII. Judge not, that ye be not judged. For with what judgment ye judge, ye shall be judged: and with what measure ye mete, it shall be measured unto you. And why beholdest thou the mote that is in thy brother's eye, but considerest not the beam that is in thine own eye? Or how wilt thou say to thy brother, Let me cast out the mote out of thine eye; and lo, the beam is in thine own eye? Thou hypocrite, cast out first the beam out of thine own eye; and then shalt thou see clearly to cast out the mote out of thy brother's eye.

Give not that which is holy unto the dogs, neither cast your pearls before the swine, lest haply they trample them under their feet, and turn and rend you.

Ask, and it shall be given you; seek, and ye shall find; knock, and it shall be opened unto you: for every one that asketh receiveth; and he that seeketh findeth; and to him that knocketh it shall be opened. Or what man is there of you, who, if his son shall ask him for a loaf, will give him a stone; or if he shall ask for a fish, will give him a serpent? If ye then, being evil, know how to give good gifts unto your children, how much more shall your Father which is in heaven give good things to them that ask Him? All things, therefore, whatsoever ye would that men should do unto you, even so do ye also unto them: for this is the Law and the Prophets.

XXIX. Though I speak with the tongues of men and of angels, and have not charity, I am become as sounding brass, or a tinkling cymbal. And though I have the gift of prophecy, and understand all mysteries, and all knowledge; and though I have all faith, so that I could remove mountains, and have not charity, I am nothing. And though I bestow all my goods to feed the poor, and though I give my body to be burned, and have not charity, it profiteth me nothing.

Charity suffereth long, and is kind: charity envieth not; charity vaunteth not itself, is not puffed up, doth not behave itself unseemly, seeketh not her own, is not easily provoked, thinketh no evil; rejoiceth not in iniquity, but rejoiceth in the truth; beareth all things, believeth all things, hopeth all things, endureth all things. Charity never faileth: but whether there be prophecies, they shall fail; whether there be tongues, they shall cease; whether there be knowledge, it shall vanish away. For we know in part, and we prophesy in part. But when that which is perfect is come, then that which is in part shall be done away. When I was a child, I spake as a child, I understood as a child, I thought as a child: but when I became a man, I put away childish things. For now we see through a glass, darkly; but then face to face: now I know in part: but then shall I know even as also I am known. And now abideth faith, hope, charity, these three; but the greatest of these is charity.

XXX. Behold what manner of love the Father hath bestowed upon us, that we should be called children of God: and such we are. For this cause the world knoweth us not, because it knew Him not. Beloved, now are we children of God, and it is not yet made manifest what we shall be. We know that, if He shall be manifested, we shall be like Him; for we shall see Him even as He is. And every one that hath this hope set on Him purifieth himself, even as He is pure.

Hereby know we love, because He laid down His life for us: and we ought to lay down our lives for the brethren. But whoso hath the world's goods, and beholdeth his brother in need, and shutteth up his compassion from him, how doth the love of God abide in him?

Beloved, let us love one another: for love is of God; and every one that loveth is begotten of God, and knoweth God. He that loveth not knoweth not God; for God is love.

Beloved, if God so loved us, we also ought to love one another. No man hath beheld God at any time: if we love one another, God abideth in us, and His love is perfected in us: hereby know we that we abide in Him, and He in us, because He hath given us of His Spirit.

And we know and have believed the love which God hath in us. God is love: and he that abideth in love abideth in God, and God abideth in him.

If a man say, I love God, and hateth his brother, he is a liar: for he that loveth not his brother whom he hath seen, cannot love God whom he hath not seen. And this commandment have we from Him, that he who loveth God love his brother also.

*c. Religion in Society and the State*

## c. Religion in Society and the State

XXXI. All the commandment which I command thee this day shall ye observe to do, that ye may live and multiply, and go in and possess the land which the Lord sware unto your fathers. And thou shalt remember all the way which the Lord thy God hath led thee these forty years in the wilderness, that He might humble thee, to prove thee, to know what was in thine heart, whether thou wouldst keep His commandments, or no. And He humbled thee, and suffered thee to hunger, and fed thee with manna, which thou knewest not, neither did thy fathers know; that He might make thee know that man doth not live by bread only, but by every thing that proceedeth out of the mouth of the Lord doth man live. Thy raiment waxed not old upon thee, neither did thy foot swell, these forty years. And thou shalt consider in thine heart, that, as a man chasteneth his son, so the Lord thy God chasteneth thee. And thou shalt keep the commandments of the Lord thy God, to walk in His ways, and to fear Him. For the Lord thy God bringeth thee into a good land, a land of brooks of water, of fountains and depths, springing forth in valleys and hills: a land of wheat and barley, and vines and fig trees and pomegranates: a land of oil olives and honey: a land wherein thou shalt eat bread without scarceness, thou shalt not lack any thing in it: a land whose stones are iron, and out of whose hills thou mayest dig brass. And thou shalt eat and be full, and thou shalt bless the Lord thy God, for the good land which He hath given thee. Beware lest thou forget the Lord thy God, in not keeping His commandments, and His judgments, and His statutes, which I command thee this day: lest when thou hast eaten and art full, and hast built goodly houses, and dwelt therein: and when thy herds and thy flocks multiply, and thy silver and thy gold is multiplied, and all that thou hast is multiplied, then thine heart be lifted up, and thou forget the Lord thy God, which brought thee forth out of the land of Egypt, out of the house of bondage; who led thee through the great and terrible wilderness, wherein were fiery serpents and scorpions, and thirsty ground where was no water; who brought thee forth water out of the rock of flint; who fed thee in the wilderness with manna, which thy fathers knew not; that He might humble thee, and that He might prove thee, to do thee good at thy latter end: and thou say in thine heart, My power and the might of mine hand hath gotten me this wealth. But thou shalt remember the Lord thy God, for it is He that giveth thee power to get wealth; that He may establish His covenant which He sware unto thy fathers, as at this day. And it shall be, if thou shalt forget the Lord thy God, and walk after other gods, and serve them, and worship them, I testify against you this day that ye shall surely perish. As the nations which the Lord maketh to perish before you, so shall ye perish; because ye would not hearken unto the voice of the Lord your God.

XXXII. At the end of every seven years thou shalt make a release. And this is the manner of the release: every creditor shall release that which he hath lent unto his neighbor; he shall not exact it of his neighbor and his brother; because the Lord's release hath been proclaimed.

Howbeit there shall be no poor with thee; (for the Lord will surely bless thee in the land which the Lord thy God giveth thee for an inheritance to possess it;) if only thou diligently hearken unto the voice of the Lord thy God, to observe to do all this commandment which I command thee this day.

If there be with thee a poor man, one of thy brethren, within any of thy gates in thy land which the Lord thy God giveth thee, thou shalt not harden thine heart, nor shut thine hand from thy poor brother: but thou shalt surely open thine hand unto him, and shalt surely lend him sufficient for his need in that which he wanteth. Beware that there be not a base thought in thine heart, saying, The seventh year, the year of release, is at hand: and thine eye be evil against thy poor brother, and thou give him nought; and he cry unto the Lord against thee, and it be sin unto thee. Thou shalt surely give him, and thine heart shall not be grieved when thou givest unto him: because that for this thing the Lord thy God shall bless thee in all thy work, and in all that thou puttest thine hand unto. For the poor shall never cease out of the land: therefore I command thee, saying, Thou shalt surely open thine hand unto thy brother, to thy needy, and to thy poor, in thy land.

XXXIII. And the Lord spake unto Moses in mount Sinai, saying, Speak unto the children of Israel, and say unto them, When ye come into the land which I give you, then shall the land keep a sabbath unto the Lord. Six years thou shalt sow thy field, and six years thou shalt prune thy vineyard, and gather in the fruits thereof; but in the seventh year shall be a sabbath of solemn rest for the land, a sabbath unto the LORD: thou shalt neither sow thy field, nor prune thy vineyard. That which groweth of itself of thy harvest thou shalt not reap, and the grapes of thy undressed vine thou shalt not gather: it shall be a year of solemn rest for the land. And the sabbath of the land shall be for food for you; for thee, and for thy servant and for thy maid, and for thy hired servant and for thy stranger that sojourn with thee; and for thy cattle, and for the beasts that are in thy land, shall all the increase thereof be for food.

And thou shalt number seven sabbaths of years unto thee, seven times seven years; and there shall be unto thee the days of seven sabbaths of years, even forty and nine years. Then shalt thou send abroad the loud trumpet on the tenth day of the seventh month; in the day of atonement shall ye send abroad the trumpet throughout all your land. And ye shall hallow the fiftieth year, and proclaim liberty throughout the land unto all the inhabitants thereof: it shall be a jubile unto you; and ye shall return every man unto his possession, and ye shall return every man unto his family. A jubile shall that fiftieth year be unto you: ye shall not sow, neither reap that which groweth of itself in it, nor gather the grapes in it of the undressed vines. For it is a jubile ; it shall be holy unto you: ye shall eat the increase thereof out of the field. In this year of jubile ye shall return every man unto his possession. And if thou sell aught unto thy neighbor, or buy of thy neighbor's hand, ye shall not wrong one another: according to the number of years after the jubile thou shalt buy of thy neighbor, and according unto the number of years of the crops he shall sell unto thee. According to the multitude of the years thou shalt increase the price thereof, and according to the fewness of the years thou shalt diminish the price of it; for the number of the crops doth he sell unto thee. And ye shall not wrong one another; but thou shalt fear thy God: for I am the Lord your God. Wherefore ye shall do My statutes, and keep My judgments and do them; and ye shall dwell in the land in safety. And the land shall yield her fruit, and ye shall eat your fill, and dwell therein in safety. And if ye shall say, What shall we eat the seventh year? behold, we shall not sow, nor gather in our increase: then I will command My blessing upon you in the sixth year, and it shall bring forth fruit for the three years. And ye shall sow the eighth year, and eat of the fruits, the old store; until the ninth year, until her fruits come in, ye shall eat the old store. And the land shall not be sold in perpetuity; for the land is Mine: for ye are strangers and sojourners with Me.

. . . . .

And if thy brother be waxen poor, and his hand fail with thee; then thou shalt uphold him: as a stranger and a sojourner shall he live with thee. Take thou no usury of him or increase; but fear thy God: that thy brother may live with thee. Thou shalt not give him thy money upon usury, nor give him thy victuals for increase. I am the Lord your God, which brought you forth out of the land of Egypt, to give you the land of Canaan, to be your God.

And if thy brother be waxen poor with thee, and sell himself unto thee; thou shalt not make him to serve as a bondservant: as an hired servant, and as a sojourner, he shall be with thee; he shall serve with thee unto the year of jubile : then shall he go out from thee, he and his children with him, and shall return unto his own family, and unto the possession of his fathers shall he return. For they are My servants which I brought forth out of the land of Egypt: they shall not be sold as bondmen. Thou shalt not rule over him with rigor; but shalt fear thy God.

XXXIV.
Give the king Thy judgments, O God,
And Thy righteousness unto the king's son.
He shall judge Thy people with righteousness,
And Thy poor with judgment.
The mountains shall bring peace to the people,
And the hills, in righteousness.

He shall judge the poor of the people,
He shall save the children of the needy,
And shall break in pieces the oppressor.
They shall fear Thee while the sun endureth,
And so long as the moon, throughout all generations.
He shall come down like rain upon the mown grass:
As showers that water the earth.
In his days shall the righteous flourish;
And abundance of peace, till the moon be no more.

.   .   .   .   .

He shall deliver the needy when he crieth;
And the poor, that hath no helper.
He shall have pity on the poor and needy,
And the souls of the needy he shall save.
He shall redeem their soul from oppression and violence;
And precious shall their blood be in his sight:
And they shall live; and to him shall be given of the gold of Sheba:
And men shall pray for him continually:
They shall bless him all the day long.
There shall be abundance of corn in the earth upon the top of the mountains;
The fruit thereof shall shake like Lebanon:

And they of the city shall flourish like grass
    of the earth.
His name shall endure forever:
His name shall be continued as long as the
    sun:
And men shall be blessed in him:
All nations shall call him happy.

    .    .    .    .    .

XXXV. And there shall come forth a shoot out of the stock of Jesse, and a branch out of his roots shall bear fruit: and the spirit of the Lord shall rest upon him, the spirit of wisdom and understanding, the spirit of counsel and might, the spirit of knowledge and of the fear of the Lord: and his delight shall be in the fear of the Lord: and he shall not judge after the sight of his eyes, neither reprove after the hearing of his ears: but with righteousness shall he judge the poor, and reprove with equity for the meek of the earth: and he shall smite the earth with the rod of his mouth, and with the breath of his lips shall he slay the wicked. And righteousness shall be the girdle of his loins, and faithfulness the girdle of his reins. And the wolf shall dwell with the lamb, and the leopard shall lie down with the kid; and the calf and

the young lion and the fatling together; and
a little child shall lead them. And the cow
and the bear shall feed; their young ones
shall lie down together: and the lion shall
eat straw like the ox. And the sucking child
shall play on the hole of the asp, and the
weaned child shall put his hand on the basil-
isk's den. They shall not hurt nor destroy
in all My holy mountain: for the earth shall
be full of the knowledge of the Lord, as the
waters cover the sea.

XXXVI. Cry aloud, spare not, lift up thy
voice like a trumpet, and declare unto My
people their transgression, and to the house
of Jacob their sins. Yet they seek Me daily,
and delight to know My ways: as a nation
that did righteousness, and forsook not the
ordinance of their God, they ask of Me
righteous ordinances, they delight to draw
near unto God. Wherefore have we fasted,
say they, and Thou seest not? wherefore have
we afflicted our soul, and Thou takest no
knowledge? Behold, in the day of your fast
ye find your own pleasure, and exact all your
labors. Behold, ye fast for strife and contention, and to smite with the fist of wickedness:
ye fast not this day so as to make your voice

to be heard on high. Is such the fast that I have chosen, the day for a man to afflict his soul? Is it to bow down his head as a rush, and to spread sackcloth and ashes under him? wilt thou call this a fast, and an acceptable day to the Lord? Is not this the fast that I have chosen? to loose the bonds of wickedness, to undo the bands of the yoke, and to let the oppressed go free, and that ye break every yoke? Is it not to deal thy bread to the hungry, and that thou bring the poor that are cast out to thy house? when thou seest the naked, that thou cover him; and that thou hide not thyself from thine own flesh? Then shall thy light break forth as the morning, and thy healing shall spring forth speedily: and thy righteousness shall go before thee: the glory of the Lord shall be thy reward. Then shalt thou call, and the Lord shall answer; thou shalt cry, and He shall say, Here I am. If thou take away from the midst of thee the yoke, the putting forth of the finger, and speaking wickedly; and if thou draw out thy soul to the hungry, and satisfy the afflicted soul; then shall thy light rise in darkness, and thine obscurity be as the noonday: and the Lord shall guide thee continually, and satisfy thy soul in dry places, and make strong thy bones; and thou shalt be like a watered garden, and like a spring of water, whose waters fail not. And they that shall be of thee shall build the old waste places: thou shalt raise up the foundations of many generations; and thou shalt be called The repairer of the breach, The restorer of paths to dwell in.

XXXVII. Four sets of views are held by men concerning property. He who says: What belongs to me shall continue to be mine, and thou shalt keep thine own, holds the common view. (Some consider this the view of the men of Sodom.) Mine shall be thine and thine shall be mine, thus say the ignorant. Mine shall be thine and thou shalt keep thine own, thus say the magnanimous. Thine shall be mine and mine shall continue to be mine, are the words of the godless.

The charitable are divided into four classes: He who gives but does not make others give, is unfriendly to the poor; he who makes others give but does not give himself, does not make the best use of his own; he who gives and makes others give, is called a pious man; but he who neither gives nor will induce others to give, is a cruel man.

There are four classes among the disciples of the wise: Sponges, funnels, sieves, and fans. Sponges sucking up all things. Funnels allowing all that is received in the one end to flow out at the other. Sieves letting the wine run through and retaining the dregs. Fans blowing off the bran and keeping the flour.

Love inspired by ulterior motives dies out when that motive disappears; but love without such motives never fades.

Judah ben Thema was in the habit of saying: Be courageous as the panther, light-winged as the eagle, swift as the deer, and strong as a lion, to do the will of thy heavenly Father.

XXXVIII. Rabbi 'Haninah, an assistant of the high-priest, said: Pray for the welfare of the government; were it not for the fear of it, men would swallow each other alive.

Rabbi Eliezer of Bartotha said: Render unto God what belongs to Him, for thou and all thou hast are His; as David said: For all things come of Thee, and of Thine own have we given Thee.

Rabbi 'Haninah ben Dosa said: He with whom the fear of God is the beginning of wisdom, his wisdom will endure. Likewise, he who is zealous in good works rather than in learning, his learning will endure.

Rabbi Elazar ben Azariah was wont to say: Without religion there can be no true culture, and without true culture there is no religion. Where there is no wisdom, there is no fear of God; and without fear of God, there is no wisdom. Without learning there can be no counsel, and without counsel there will be lack of learning. Where there is a dearth of bread, learning cannot thrive, and lack of learning causes dearth of bread.

*d.* Responsive Readings

## d. Responsive Readings

XXXIX.

*Minister.*—Happy are they who dwell in Thy house, they shall continually praise Thee.

*People.*—Happy are they who thus know Him; happy the people whose God is the Eternal.

*M.*—I will extol Thee, my God, O King, and I will bless Thy name forever and ever.

*P.*—Every day I will bless Thee, and I will praise Thy name forever and ever.

*M.*—Great is the Lord and highly to be praised; His greatness is unsearchable.

*P.*—One generation shall praise Thy works to another, and shall declare Thy mighty deeds.

*M.*—I will speak of the glorious honor of Thy majesty, and of Thy wonderful works.

*P.*—And men shall speak of the might of Thy deeds, and shall declare Thy greatness.

*M.*—They shall remember Thy great goodness, and sing of Thy righteousness.

*P.*—The Lord is gracious and full of compassion, slow to anger, and rich in mercy.

*M.*—The Lord is good to all, and His tender mercies are over all His works.

*P.*—All Thy works praise Thee, O God, and Thy holy ones bless Thee.

*M.*—They proclaim the glory of Thy Kingdom, and speak of Thy power.

*P.*—Thy kingdom is an everlasting Kingdom, and Thy dominion endureth forever.

*M.*—The Lord upholdeth the falling, and uplifteth those who are bowed down.

*P.*—The eyes of all wait upon Thee, and Thou givest them their food in due season.

*M.*—Thou openest Thy hand and satisfiest the desire of every living being.

*P.*—The Lord is righteous in all His ways, and merciful in all His works.

*M.*—The Lord is near to all who call upon Him, who call upon Him in truth.

*P.*—He fulfilleth the desire of those that fear Him; He will hear their cry and save them.

*M.*—My mouth shall praise the Lord; and let all flesh bless His name forever and ever.

*P.*—Let us praise the Lord henceforth and forever, Hallelujah!

XL.

*Minister.*—O Lord! Thou hast searched me and known me! Thou understandest my thoughts from afar!

*People.*—Thou seest my path and my lying-down, and art acquainted with all my ways!

*M.*—For before the word is upon my tongue, behold, O Lord! Thou knowest it altogether!

*P.*—Thou besettest me behind and before, and layest Thy hand upon me!

*M.*—Such knowledge is too wonderful for me; it is high, I cannot attain to it!

*P.*—Whither shall I go from Thy spirit, and whither shall I flee from Thy presence?

*M.*—If I ascend into heaven, Thou art there! If I descend into the underworld, behold, Thou art there!

*P.*—If I take the wings of the morning, and dwell in the remotest parts of the sea,
*M.*—Even there, shall Thy hand lead me, and Thy right hand shall hold me!
*P.*—If I say, Surely the darkness shall cover me; even the night shall be light about me.
*M.*—Yea, the darkness hideth not from Thee, but the night shineth as the day.
*P.*—The darkness and the light are both alike to Thee!
*M.*—I will praise Thee; for I am wonderfully made; marvellous are Thy works, and this my soul knoweth full well!
*P.*—In Thy book was everything written; my days were appointed before one of them existed.
*M.*—How precious to me are Thy thoughts, O God! how great is the sum of them!
*P.*—If I should count them, they would outnumber the sand; when I awake, I am still with Thee!
*M.*—Search me, O God! and know my heart; try me, and know my thoughts;
*P.*—And see if the way of trouble be within me, and lead me in the way of everlasting!

## XLI.

*Minister.*—Truly, my soul waiteth upon God, from Him cometh my help.

*People.*—God is my refuge and my glory; He is my strength and my safety.

*M.*—Trust in Him at all times, pour out your hearts before Him.

*P.*—Commit thy ways unto the Lord and He will order all things well.

*M.*—Show me Thy way, O Lord, teach me Thy paths and lead me in Thy truth.

*P.*—Whom have I in heaven but Thee, and there is none upon earth that I desire beside Thee.

*M.*—When my flesh and my heart fail, God is still my strength and my portion forever.

*P.*—Wait on the Lord, be of good courage and He shall strengthen thy heart.

*M.*—Create in me a pure heart and renew a right spirit within me.

*P.*—When many thoughts perplex me, Thy comforts delight my soul.

*M.*—My times are in Thy hands, and Thou wilt sustain me even unto the end.

*P.*—How precious is Thy loving-kindness, O God, therefore the children of men hide under Thy wings.

*M.*—With Thee is the fountain of life; in Thy light shall we see light.

*P.*—Continue Thy mercy unto them that know Thee, and Thy righteousness to the upright in heart.

XLII.

*Minister.*—Happy are they who dwell in Thy house, they shall continually praise Thee.

*People.*—Happy are they who thus know Him; happy the people whose God is the Eternal.

*M.*—I will extol Thee, my God, O King, and I will bless Thy name forever and ever.

*P.*—Every day I will bless Thee, and I will praise Thy name forever and ever.

*M.*—Great is the Lord and highly to be praised; His greatness is unsearchable.

*P.*—One generation shall praise Thy works to another, and shall declare Thy mighty deeds.

*M.*—I will speak of the glorious honor of Thy majesty, and of Thy wonderful works.

*P.*—And men shall speak of the might of Thy deeds, and shall declare Thy greatness.

*M.*—They shall remember Thy great goodness, and sing of Thy righteousness.

*P.*—The Lord is gracious and full of compassion, slow to anger, and rich in mercy.

*M.*—When many thoughts perplex me, Thy comforts delight my soul.

*P.*—My times are in Thy hands, and Thou wilt sustain me even unto the end.

XLIII.

*Minister.*—Be not anxious for your life, what ye shall eat, . . . nor yet for your body, what ye shall put on. Is not the life more than the food, and the body than the raiment?

*People.*—Work not for the meat which perisheth, but for the meat which abideth into eternal life.

*M.*—The lamp of the body is the eye: if therefore thine eye be single, thy whole body shall be full of light.

*P.*—But if thine eye be evil, thy whole body shall be full of darkness.

*M.*—No man can serve two masters: for either he will hate the one and love the other; or else he will hold to one and despise the other.

*P.*—Ye cannot serve God and mammon.

*M.*—Take heed, and keep yourselves from all covetousness: for a man's life consisteth not in the abundance of the things which he possesseth.

*P.*—It is more blessed to give than to receive.

*M.*—Blessed are the meek: for they shall inherit the earth.

*P.*—Take my yoke upon you, and learn of me; for I am meek and lowly in heart.

*M.*—Blessed are the poor in spirit: for their's is the kingdom of heaven.

*P.*—If thy brother sin against thee seven times in the day, and seven times turn again to thee, saying I repent; thou shalt forgive him.

*M.*—Blessed are the merciful: for they shall obtain mercy.

*P.*—He that is greatest among you shall be your servant. If any man would be first, he shall be last of all, and minister of all.

*M.*—Be ye merciful, even as your Father is merciful.

*P.*—Love your enemies, and do them good, and lend, despairing of no man.

*M.*—Let your loins be girded about, and your lamps burning; and be ye yourselves

like unto men looking for their lord,
when he shall return from the marriage
feast; that, when he cometh and knocketh, they may straightway open to him.

*P.*—Blessed are those servants whom the
Lord when He cometh shall find watching.

*M.*—He that is faithful in a very little is
faithful also in much: and he that is
unrighteous in a very little is unrighteous also in much.

*P.*—I must work the works of Him that sent
me, while it is day: the night cometh,
when no man can work.

*M.*—Blessed are the pure in heart: for they
shall see God.

*P.*—Except ye turn, and become as little
children, ye shall in no wise enter into
the kingdom of heaven. Whosoever
therefore shall humble himself as this
little child, the same is the greatest in
the kingdom of heaven.

*M.*—Peace I leave with you; my peace I
give unto you: not as the world giveth,
give I unto you.

*P.*—These things have I spoken unto you,
that my joy may be in you, and that
your joy may be fulfilled.

*M.*—Blessed are they that have been persecuted for righteousness' sake: for their's is the kingdom of heaven.

*P.*—A new commandment I give unto you, that ye love one another; even as I have loved you, that ye also love one another.

*M.*—The kingdom of God cometh not with observation: neither shall they say, Lo, here! or, There! for lo! the kingdom of God is within you.

*P.*—Except a man be born anew, he cannot see the kingdom of God.

# B. Ethnic Scriptures

[*Hindu, Persian, Chinese, Egyptian, Buddhist, Grecian, Roman, and Mohammedan*]

## a. Universality in Religion

# B. Ethnic Scriptures

[*Hindu, Persian, Chinese, Egyptian, Buddhist, Grecian, Roman, and Mohammedan*]

## a. Universality in Religion

XLIV. Be thy creed or thy prayers what they may, unless thou hast truth within thee, thou wilt not find the path to true happiness. He in whom the truth dwells is twice born.

Any place where the mind of man can be undisturbed is suitable for the worship of the Supreme Being.

Foolish are they who are perpetually inquiring where the Deity resides. God dwells in all things in His fulness. Kine are of different colors, but all milk is white. The flowers on altars are of many species, but all worship is one. Systems of faith are different, but God is one.

The object of all religions is alike. All men seek the object of their love, and all the world is love's dwelling.

Why talk of a mosque or church? He alone is a true Hindu whose heart is just; and he alone is a true Mohammedan whose life is true.

The Supreme Being is sometimes with him who counts his prayers on sacred beads in the mosque, and sometimes with him who bows down before idols in the temple. He is the friend of the Hindu, the intimate of the Mohammedan, the companion of the Christian, and the confidant of the Jew.

Heaven is a palace with many doors, and each one may enter in his own way.

XLV. If thou art a Mussulman, go stay with the Franks; if a Christian, join the Jews; if a Shiah, mix with the schismatics: whatever thy religion, associate with men of opposite persuasion. If in hearing their discourses thou art not in the least moved, but canst mix with them freely, thou hast attained peace, and art a master of creation.

Háfiz says: The object of all religions is alike. All men seek their beloved; and all the world is love's dwelling: why talk of a mosque or a church?

Diversity of worship has divided the human race into seventy-two nations. From among all their dogmas I have selected one,—Divine Love.

All nations and languages repeat the name of God, even infancy lisps it,—Allah, Tangarí, Yezdán, Elohim. Yet cannot His praise be duly expressed by mortal till the dumb man shall be eloquent, and stocks and stones find a voice; till the silent universe rejoices in language.

Which is the great name of God?

Communicate to me His least name and I will return to thee His greatest. Every day He is in action: one day of His is equal to a thousand years of man's. O Thou whose light manifests itself in the vesture of the world! Thy names are manifested in the nature of man; Thy knowledge shows itself in the science of Thy prophets; Thy bounty is manifested in the bounty of great hearts. Recognize the mark of God in every place, and never place the foot without its own limit. The world is the image of God.

Look not askance ; the Holy One will ever
    be the same,
The God of all, though oft invoked by many
    a different name.

Whatever road I take joins the highway that leads to Thee.

He needs no other rosary whose thread of life is strung with beads of love and thought.

Nánác lay on the ground, absorbed in devotion, with his feet towards Mecca. A Moslem priest seeing him cried, Base infidel! how dar'st thou turn thy feet towards the house of Allah ? Nánác answered, And thou —turn them if thou canst towards any spot where the awful house of God is *not!*

Every soul that maketh choice of justice shall attain unto God.

Every prophet whom I send goeth forth to establish religion, not to root it up.

XLVI. For a week Abraham would scarce break his fast for fear some hungry traveller might pass needing his store. Daily he looked out upon the desert, and on a day he beheld the bent form of an aged man, his hair white as snow, tottering toward his door. "Guest of mine eyes," said Abraham, "enter thou with welcome, and be pleased to share my bread and salt." The stranger entered, and to him was given the place of honor. When the cloth was spread, and the family had gathered round the board, each uttered "Bismillah" ("In the name of God") save one: the aged guest uttered no word. Abraham said: "Old man, is it not right when thou dost eat thy food to repeat the name of God?" The stranger said, "My custom is that of the fire-worshipper." Then Abraham arose in wrath, and drove the aged Geber from his house. Even as he did so a swift-winged spirit stood before the patriarch and said: "Abraham! for a hundred years the divine bounty has flowed out in sunshine and rain, in bread and life, to this man: is it for thee to withhold thy hand from him because his worship is not thine?"

XLVII. God's is the east and the west,

and wherever ye turn there is God's face; verily, God comprehends and knows.

Every sect has some one side to which they turn (in prayer); but do ye hasten onwards to good works; wherever ye are God will bring you all together; verily, God is mighty over all.

Righteousness is not that ye turn your faces towards the east or the west, but righteousness is, one who believes in God, and the last day, and the angels, and the Book, and the prophets, and who gives wealth for His love to kindred, and orphans, and the poor, and the son of the road, and beggars, and those in captivity; and who is steadfast in prayer, and gives alms; and those who are sure of their covenant when they make a covenant; and the patient in poverty, and distress, and in time of violence; these are they who are true, and these are those who fear.

For every nation have we made rites which they observe; let them not then dispute about the matter, but call upon thy Lord; verily, thou art surely in a right guidance!

God's is the kingdom of the heavens and the earth, and on the day when the Hour shall arise on that day shall those who call it vain be losers. And thou shalt see each nation kneeling, each nation summoned to its Book, "To-day are ye rewarded for that which ye have done."

XLVIII. We believe in God, and in that which has been sent to us; also in that which has been sent to Abraham, and Ismael, and Isaac, and Jacob, and the Tribes; and in that which has been given to Moses and to Jesus; and in that which was given to all the prophets from their Lord.

Will ye dispute with us about God? He is our Lord and your Lord. We will answer with our actions, and you shall answer with yours. In God we place our reliance.

All have a quarter of the heavens to which they turn. Both the East and the West belong to God; therefore, whichever way ye turn, there is God.

Nothing has been said to thee which hath not been said of old to apostles before thee. Thou wilt see every nation kneeling. To its own Book shall every nation be summoned.

The Jews and Christians say they are sons

of God; that they are His beloved. Nay, they are but a part of the men whom He hath made. To every one has been given a rule and a beaten road.

If God had pleased, He would surely have made you all one people; but He would test you by what He has given to each.

Whatever ye be, prove yourselves emulous in good deeds. God will one day bring you all together. To God shall ye all return, and He will enlighten you concerning the subjects of your disputes.

Jesus came and abolished the law of Moses. Mohammed followed him, and introduced his five prayers a day. The followers of both these say that after their prophet no other is to be expected; and they occupy themselves talking thus idly from morning to evening.

But, meanwhile, you who are living under one of these dispensations, tell me, Do you enjoy the sun and the moon more than others? or less than others?

If thou art a Mussulman, go stay with the Franks. If thou art a Christian, mix with the Jews. If thou art a Shiah, mix with the schismatics. Whatever is thy religion, associate with men of opposite persuasions. If thou canst mix with them freely, and art not the least moved while listening to their discourse, thou hast attained peace, and art a master of creation.

## b. Ethical and Spiritual Religion

## b. Ethical and Spiritual Religion

XLIX. Who is the God to whom we shall offer sacrifice?

He who gives breath, He who gives strength, whose command all the bright gods revere, whose shadow is immortality, whose shadow is death:—Who is the God to whom we shall offer sacrifice?

He who through His might became the sole King of the breathing and twinkling world, who governs all this, man and beast:—Who is the God to whom we shall offer sacrifice?

He through whose might these snowy mountains are, and the sea, they say, with the distant river, He of whom these regions are indeed the two arms:—Who is the God to whom we shall offer sacrifice?

He through whom the awful heaven and the earth were made fast, He through whom the ether was established, and the firmament;

He who measured the air in the sky:—Who is the God to whom we shall offer sacrifice?

He to whom heaven and earth, standing firm by His will, look up, trembling in their mind; He over whom the risen sun shines forth:—Who is the God to whom we shall offer sacrifice?

· · · · ·

He who by His might looked even over the waters which held power (the germ) and generated the sacrifice (light), He who alone is God above all gods:—Who is the God to whom we shall offer sacrifice?

L. All this is Brahman. Let a man meditate on that (visible world) as beginning, ending, and breathing in it (the Brahman).

Now man is a creature of will. According to what his will is in this world, so will he be when he has departed this life. Let him therefore have this will and belief:

The intelligent, whose body is spirit, whose form is light, whose thoughts are true, whose nature is like ether (omnipresent and invisible), from whom all works, all desires, all sweet odors and tastes proceed; He who embraces all this, who never speaks and is never surprised.

He is my Self within the heart, smaller than a corn of rice, smaller than a corn of barley, smaller than a mustard seed, smaller than a canary seed or the kernel of a canary seed. He also is my Self within the heart, greater than the earth, greater than the sky, greater than heaven, greater than all these worlds.

He from whom all works, all desires, all sweet odors and tastes proceed, who embraces all this, who never speaks and who is never surprised, he, my Self within the heart, is that Brahman. When I shall have departed from hence, I shall obtain Him (that Self). He who has this faith has no doubt.

LI. Those who depart from hence without having discovered the Self and those true desires, for them there is no freedom in all the worlds. But those who depart from hence, after having discovered the Self and those true desires, for them there is freedom in all the worlds.

Pragapati said: The Self which is free from sin, free from old age, from death and grief, from hunger and thirst, which desires nothing but what it ought to desire, and imagines nothing but what it ought to imagine, that it is which we must search out, that it is which we must try to understand. He who has searched out that Self and understands it, obtains all worlds and all desires.

All this, whatsoever moves on earth, is to be hidden in the Lord (the Self). When thou hast surrendered all this, then thou mayest enjoy.

When to a man who understands, the Self has become all things, what sorrow, what trouble can there be to him who once beheld that unity?

LII. Maghavat, this body is mortal and always held by death. It is the abode of that Self which is immortal and without body. When in the body (by thinking this body is I and I am this body), the Self is held by pleasure and pain. So long as he is in the body, he cannot get free from pleasure and pain. But when he is free of the body (when he knows himself different from the body), then neither pleasure nor pain touches him.

The wind is without body, the cloud, lightning, and thunder are without body (without hands, feet, etc.). Now as these, arising from this heavenly ether (space), appear in their own form, as soon as they have approached the highest light, thus does that serene being, arising from this body, appear in its own form, as soon as it has approached the highest light (the knowledge of Self). He (in that state) is the highest person.

. . . . . .

He who knows, let me think this, he is the Self, the mind is his divine eye. He, the Self, seeing these pleasures (which to others are hidden like a buried treasure of gold) through his divine eye, *i. e.*, the mind, rejoices.

This (body) indeed withers and dies when the living Self has left it; the living Self dies not.

LIII. "Fetch me from thence a fruit of the Nyagrodha tree."
"Here is one, Sir."
"Break it."
"It is broken, Sir."
"What do you see there?"

" These seeds, almost infinitesimal."
" Break one of them."
" It is broken, Sir."
" What do you see there ? "
" Not anything, Sir."
The father said: " My son, that subtile essence which you do not perceive there, of that very essence this great Nyagrodha tree exists.

" Believe it, my son. That which is the subtile essence, in it all that exists has its self. It is the True. It is the Self, and thou, O Svetaketu, art it."

The wise, when he knows that that by which he perceives all objects in sleep or in waking is the great omnipresent Self, grieves no more.

LIV. Now that golden person, who is seen within the sun, with golden beard and golden hair, golden altogether to the very tips of his nails, Him they see in this earth, in heaven, in the air, in the ether, in the water, in herbs, in trees, in the moon, in the stars, in all beings. Him alone they call Brahman.

And the ether which is around us is the

same as the ether which is within us. And the ether which is within us, that is the ether within the heart. That ether within the heart (as Brahman) is omnipresent and unchanging. He who knows this obtains omnipresent and unchangeable happiness.

Now that light which shines above this heaven, higher than all, higher than everything, in the highest world, beyond which there are no other worlds, that is the same light which is within man.

Those who belong to us, whether living or departed, and whatever else there is which we wish for and do not obtain, all that we find there (if we descend into our heart, where Brahman dwells, in the ether of the heart).

Let him know that the person within all beings, not heard here, not reached, not thought, not subdued, not seen, not understood, not classed, but hearing, thinking, seeing, classing, sounding, understanding, knowing, is his Self.

LV. The wise who, by means of meditation

on his Self, recognizes the Ancient, who is difficult to be seen, who has entered into the dark, who is hidden in the cave, who dwells in the abyss, as God, he indeed leaves joy and sorrow far behind.

And indeed to him who thus knows this Brahma-upanishad (the secret doctrine of the Veda) the sun does not rise and does not set. For him there is day, once and for all.

The teacher said : Friend, you shine like one who knows Brahman.

There is one ruler, the Self within all things, who makes the one form manifold. The wise who perceive him within their Self, to them belongs eternal happiness, not to others.

He, the highest Person, who is awake in us while we are asleep, shaping one lovely sight after another, that indeed is the Bright, that is Brahman, that alone is called the Immortal. All worlds are contained in it, and no one goes beyond.

He who knows that highest Brahman, becomes even Brahman. In his race no one is born ignorant of Brahman. He overcomes grief, he overcomes evil; free from the fetters of the heart, he becomes immortal.

He who is this (Brahman) in man, and he who is that (Brahman) in the sun, both are one.

Adoration to the Highest Self. Hari, Om!
Verily, in the beginning all this was Self, one only; there was nothing else living whatsoever.
He thought: Shall I send forth worlds?
He sent forth these worlds.

LVI. The True God is to all beings as honey, to Him all beings are as honey. That immortal, glorious person abideth in all truth, is holy and intelligent, is full of light and reality. He is the God for all the Soul of all. He is the Immortal, He is the Brahma.

I think not I have known God, nor think I that I do not know God. He who thinks he knoweth not God, and yet thinks he knoweth God, hath truly known Him.

God revealeth Himself in all things as the Life of all. The wise man sayeth nought in forgetfulness of Him. The wise man disporteth in Him, enjoyeth in Him, and is full of good deeds. He is chief among the worshippers of God.

In the abode of heaven, O Death, there is no fear, neither art thou there, nor the fear of disease. Living beyond both hunger and thirst, the soul is delivered from sorrow, and liveth joyfully in heaven.

The great, vast Being is the Lord of All and the dispenser of all hearts. This glorious, wise, eternal God doth dispense all pure, immaculate conditions of life.

LVII. O son of Prithâ! now hear how you can without doubt know Me fully, fixing your mind on Me, and resting in Me, and practising devotion. . . . Among thousands of men, only some work for perfection; and even of those who have reached perfection, and who are assiduous, only some know Me truly. Earth, water, fire, air, space, mind, understanding, and egoism, thus is My nature divided eightfold. . . . Know that all things have these (for their) source. I am the producer and the destroyer of the whole universe. There is nothing else, O Dhanañgaya! higher than Myself; all this is woven upon Me, like numbers of pearls upon a thread. I am the taste in water, O son of Kuntî! I am the light of the sun and moon. I am "Om" in all the Vedas, sound in space, and manliness in human beings; I am the fragrant smell in the earth, refulgence in the fire; I am life in all beings, and penance in those who perform penance. Know Me, O son of Prithâ! to be the eternal seed of all beings; I am the discernment of the discerning ones, and I am the glory of the glorious. . . . I am love unopposed to piety among all beings. . . . To the man of knowledge I am dear above all things and he is dear to me. . . .

I am the father of this universe, the mother, the creator, the thing to be known, the means of sanctification, the goal, the sustainer, the lord, the supervisor, the residence, the asylum, the friend, the source, and that in which it merges, the support, the receptacle, and the inexhaustible seed. . . .

Coming to this transient unhappy world, worship Me. (Place your) mind on Me, become My devotee, my worshipper; reverence Me, and thus making Me your highest goal, and devoting yourself to abstraction, you will certainly come to Me.

LVIII. Whichever form (of Deity) any worshipper wishes to worship with faith, to that form I render his faith steady. Possessed of that faith, he seeks to propitiate (the Deity in) that (form), and obtains from it those beneficial things which he desires, (though they are) really given by Me. . . . Those who worship the divinities go to the divinities, and My worshippers, too, go to Me. The undiscerning ones, not knowing My transcendent and inexhaustible essence, than which there is nothing higher, think Me, who am unperceived, to have become perceptible. Surrounded by the delusion of My mystic power, I am not manifest to all. This deluded world knows not Me unborn and inexhaustible. I know, O Arguna! the things which have been, those which are, and those which are to be. But Me nobody knows. . . . Those who, resting on Me, work for release from old age and death, know the Brahman, the whole Adhyâtma, and all action.

## LIX.

In my heart I place the feet,
The golden feet of God.
If He be mine, what can I need?
My God is everywhere:
Within, beyond man's highest word,
My God existeth still:
In sacred books, in darkest night,
In deepest, bluest sky,
In those who know the truth, and in
The faithful few on earth.

LX. The law of Mazda, O Spitama Zarathustra! cleanses the faithful from every evil thought, word and deed, as a swift-rushing mighty wind cleanses the plain.

The will of the Lord is the law of holiness.

There is many a one, O holy Zarathustra! said Ahura Mazda, who wears a mouth-veil, but who has not girded his loins with the law; do not call him an Athravan, O holy Zarathustra! Thus said Ahura Mazda.

Him thou shalt call an Athravan, O holy

Zarathustra! who throughout the night sits up and demands of the holy wisdom, which makes man free from anxiety, with dilated heart, and cheerful at the head of the Kinvat bridge, and which makes him reach that world, that holy world, that excellent world, the world of paradise.

(Therefore) demand of Me, thou upright one! of Me, who am the Maker, the best of all beings, the most knowing, the most pleased in answering what is asked of Me; demand of Me, that thou mayest be the better, that thou mayest be the happier.

The holy Zarathustra said aloud: This I ask Thee: teach me the truth, O LORD!

Holiness is the best of all good. Happy, happy the man who is holy with perfect holiness!

LXI. I think thus in my heart:
Should the evil thoughts of the earthly man be a hundred times worse, they would not rise so high as the good thoughts of the heavenly Mithra;
Should the evil words of the earthly man be a hundred times worse, they would not

rise so high as the good words of the heavenly Mithra;

Should the evil deeds of the earthly man be a hundred times worse, they would not rise so high as the good deeds of the heavenly Mithra.

The first step that the soul of the faithful man made placed him in the Good-Thought Paradise;

The second step that the soul of the faithful man made placed him in the Good-Word Paradise;

The third step that the soul of the faithful man made placed him in the Good-Deed Paradise.

When shall the (Divine) Righteousness, the Good Mind (of the Lord, and His) Sovereign Power (come) hastening to me (to give me strength for my task and mission), O Great Creator, the Living Lord!

O (thou Divine) Righteousness, and thou Benevolent Mind (of Deity)! I will worship You, and Ahura Mazda the first, for all of whom the pious ready mind (within us) is causing the imperishable kingdom to advance.

(And) do thou, O (Divine) Righteousness, bestow (upon me) that sacred blessing which is constituted by the attainments of the Good Mind (within my soul).

LXII. This I ask Thee, O Ahura! tell me aright: Who by generation was the first father of the Righteous Order (within the world)? Who gave the (recurring) sun and stars their (undeviating) way? Who established that whereby the moon waxes and whereby she wanes, save Thee? These things, O Great Creator! would I know, and others likewise still.

This I ask Thee, O Ahura! tell me aright: Who from beneath hath sustained the earth and the clouds above that they do not fall? Who made the waters and the plants? Who to the wind has yoked on the storm-clouds, the swift and fleetest two? Who, O Great Creator! is the inspirer of the good thoughts (within our souls)?

.   .   .   .   .

This I ask Thee, O Ahura! tell me aright: Who fashioned Aramaiti (our piety) the beloved, together with Thy Sovereign Power? Who, through his guiding wisdom, hath made the son revering the father? (Who made him beloved?) With (questions such as) these, so abundant, O Mazda! I press Thee, O bountiful Spirit, (Thou) maker of all!

.   .   .   .   .

This I ask Thee, O Ahura! tell me aright: How to myself shall I hallow the Faith of Thy people, which the beneficent kingdom's Lord hath taught me, even the admonition which He called Thine equal hath taught me through His lofty (and most righteous Sovereignty and) Power, as He dwells in like abode with Thine Order and Thy Good Mind?

.   .   .   .   .

This I ask Thee, O Ahura! tell me aright: How shall I deliver that Demon-of-the-Lie into the two hands of Thine Order (as he lives in our hosts) to cast her down to death through Thy Māthras of doctrine, and to send mighty destruction among her evil believers, to keep those deceitful and harsh oppressors from reaching their (fell) aims?

LXIII. Once upon a time the fishes of a certain river took counsel together, and said: "They tell us that our life and being is from the water, but we have never seen water, and know not what it is." Then some among them wiser than the rest said: "We have heard that there dwelleth in the sea a very wise and learned fish who knoweth all things; let us journey to him, and ask him to show us water, or explain unto us what it is." So several of their number set out upon their travels, and at last came to the sea wherein this sage fish resided. On hearing their request he answered them thus:

> " O ye who seek to solve the knot!
> Ye live in God, yet know Him not.
> Ye sit upon the river's brink,
>   Yet crave in vain a drop to drink.
> Ye dwell beside a countless store,
> Yet perish hungry at the door."

LXIV. The sage does not accumulate (for himself). The more that he expends for others, the more does he possess of his own; the more that he gives to others, the more does he have himself.

 . . . . .

The true men of old knew nothing of the love of life or of the hatred of death. Entrance into life occasioned them no joy; the exit from it awakened no resistance.

Composedly they went and came. They did not forget what their beginning had been, and they did not inquire into what their end would be. They accepted (their life) and rejoiced in it; they forgot (all fear of death), and returned (to their state before life).

. . . . .

What was anciently called " the Attainment of the Aim " did not mean the getting of carriages and coronets; it simply meant that nothing more was needed for their enjoyment. Nowadays what is called " the Attainment of the Aim " means the getting of carriages and coronets. But carriages and coronets belong to the body; they do not affect the nature as it is constituted. When such things happen to come, it is but for a time; being but for a time, their coming cannot be obstructed and their going cannot be stopped. Therefore we should not because of carriages and coronets indulge our aims, nor because of distress and straitness resort to the vulgar (learning and thinking); the one of these conditions and the other may equally conduce to our enjoyment, which is simply to be free from anxiety. If now the departure of what is transient takes away one's enjoyment, this view shows that what enjoyment it had given was worthless. Hence it is said: They who lose themselves in their pursuit of things, and lose their nature in their study of what is vulgar, must be pronounced people who turn things upside down.

LXV. He who understands the conditions of life does not strive after what is of no use to life; and he who understands the conditions of destiny does not strive after what is beyond the reach of knowledge. In nourishing the body it is necessary to have beforehand the things (appropriate to its support); but there are cases where there is a superabundance of such things, and yet the body is not nourished. In order to have life it is necessary that it have not left the body; but there are cases when the body has not been left by it, and yet the life has perished.

When life comes, it cannot be declined; when it goes, it cannot be detained. Alas! the men of the world think that to nourish the body is sufficient to preserve life; and when such nourishment is not sufficient to preserve the life, what can be done in the world that will be sufficient? Though (all that men can do) will be insufficient, yet there are things which they feel they ought to do, and they do not try to avoid doing them. For those who wish to avoid caring for the body, their best plan is to abandon the world. Abandoning the world, they are free from its entanglements. Free from its entanglements, their (minds) are correct and their (temperament) is equable. Thus correct and equable, they succeed in securing a renewal of life, as some have done. In securing a renewal of life, they are not far from the True (Secret of their being). But how is it sufficient to abandon worldly affairs? and how is it sufficient to forget the (business of) life? Through the renouncing of (worldly) affairs, the body has no more toil; through forgetting the (business of) life, the vital power suffers no diminution. When the body is completed and the vital power is restored (to its original vigor), the man is one with Heaven. Heaven and Earth are the father and mother of all things. It is by their union that the body is formed; it is by their separation that a (new) beginning is brought about. When the body and vital power suffer no diminution, we have what may be called the transference of power. From the vital force there comes another more vital, and man returns to be the assistant of Heaven.

LXVI. He whose mind is thus grandly fixed emits a heavenly light. In him who emits this heavenly light men see the (true) man. When a man has cultivated himself (up to this point), thenceforth he remains constant in himself. When he is thus constant in himself (what is merely) the human element will leave him, but Heaven will help him. Those whom their human element has left we call the people of Heaven. Those whom Heaven helps we call the Sons of Heaven. Those who would by learning attain to this seek for what they cannot learn. Those who would by effort attain to this, attempt what effort can never effect. Those who aim by reasoning to reach it reason where reasoning has no place. To know to stop where they cannot arrive by means of knowledge is the highest attainment. Those who cannot do this will be destroyed on the lathe of Heaven.

The Tower of Intelligence has its Guardian, who acts unconsciously, and whose care will not be effective, if there be any conscious purpose in it. If one who has not this entire sincerity in himself make any outward demonstration, every such demonstration will be incorrect. The thing will enter into him, and not let go its hold. Then with every fresh demonstration there will be still greater failure. If he do what is not good in the light of open day, men will have the opportunity of punishing him; if he do it in darkness and secrecy, spirits will inflict the punishment. Let a man understand this— his relation both to men and spirits — and then he will do what is good in the solitude of himself.

LXVII. He whose rule of life is in himself does not act for the sake of a name. He whose rule is outside himself has his will set on extensive acquisition. He who does not act for the sake of a name emits a light even in his ordinary conduct; he whose will is set on extensive acquisition is but a trafficker.

The greatest politeness is to show no special respect to others; the greatest righteousness is to take no account of things; the greatest wisdom is to lay no plans; the greatest benevolence is to make no demonstration of affection; the greatest good faith is to give no pledge of sincerity.

Repress the impulses of the will; unravel the errors of the mind; put away the entanglements to virtue; and clear away all that obstructs the free course of the Tâo.

. . . . .

A man's proper Truth is pure sincerity in its highest degree; without this pure sincerity one cannot move others.

. . . . .

Not to be separate from his primal source constitutes what we call the Heavenly man; not to be separate from the essential nature thereof constitutes what we call the Spirit-like man; not to be separate from its real truth constitutes what we call the Perfect man.

LXVIII. The feet of man on the earth tread but on a small space, but going on to where he has not trod before, he traverses a great distance easily; so his knowledge is but small, but going on to what he does not already know, he comes to know what is meant by Heaven. He knows it as The Great Unity; The Great Mystery; The Great Illuminator; The Great Framer; The Great Boundlessness; The Great Truth; The

Great Determiner. This makes his knowledge complete. As The Great Unity, he comprehends it; as The Great Mystery, he unfolds it; as The Great Illuminator, he contemplates it; as The Great Framer, it is to him the Cause of all; as The Great Boundlessness, all is to him its embodiment; as The Great Truth, he examines it; as The Great Determiner, he holds it fast.

Thus Heaven is to him all; accordance with it is the brightest intelligence.

LXIX. Dissatisfied (continued his argument), saying: "In thus thinking it necessary for their reputation, they bitterly distressed their bodies, denied themselves what was pleasant, and restricted themselves to a bare sustenance in order to sustain their life; but so they had lifelong distress, and long-continued pressure till their death arrived." Know-the-Mean replied: "Tranquil ease is happiness; a superfluity is injurious—so it is with all things, and especially it is so, where the superfluity is of wealth. The ears of the rich are provided with the music of bells, drums, flageolets, and flutes; and their mouths are stuffed with the flesh of fed beasts and with wine of the richest flavor;

so are their desires satisfied, till they forget their proper business:—theirs may be pronounced a condition of disorder. Sunk deeply in their self-sufficiency, they resemble individuals ascending a height with a heavy burden on their backs:—their condition may be pronounced one of bitter suffering. They covet riches, thinking to derive comfort from them; they covet power, and would fain monopolize it; when quiet and retired, they are drowned in luxurious indulgence; their persons seem to shine, and they are full of boasting:—they may be said to be in a state of disease. In their desire to be rich and striving for gain, they fill their stores, and, deaf to all admonition, refuse to desist from their course. They are even more elated, and hold on their way:— their conduct may be pronounced disgraceful. When their wealth is amassed till they cannot use it, they clasp it to their breasts and will not part with it; when their hearts are distressed with their very fulness, they still seek for more and will not desist:—their condition may be said to be sad. Indoors they are apprehensive of pilfering and begging thieves, and out-of-doors they are afraid of being injured by plundering robbers; indoors they have many chambers and partitions, and out-of-doors they do not dare to go alone:—they may be said to be in a state of (constant) alarm."

These six conditions are the most deplorable in the world, but they forget them all, and have lost their faculty of judgment. When the evil comes, though they begged it with all the powers of their nature, and by the sacrifice of all their wealth, they could not bring back one day of untroubled peace. When they look for their reputation, it is not to be seen; when they seek for their wealth, it is not to be got. To task their thoughts, and destroy their bodies, striving for (such an end as) this;—is it not a case of great delusion?

LXX. Now filial piety is the root of (all) virtue, and (the stem) out of which grows (all moral) teaching.

. . . . .

Morning and night be reverent. Be upright, be pure.

. . . . .

Pride brings loss, and humility receives increase;—this is the way of Heaven.

. . . . .

From Heaven are the (social) relationships with their several duties.

* * * * *

The superior man rests in this,—that he will indulge in no luxurious ease.

* * * * *

Want of harmony (in the life) rises from (the want of it in) one's (inner) self;—strive to be harmonious.

* * * * *

In its inspection of men below, Heaven's first consideration is of their righteousness, and it bestows on them (accordingly) length of years or the contrary.

* * * * *

Do not speak lightly; your words are your own.

* * * * *

Early and late never be but earnest. If you do not attend jealously to your small actions, the result will be to affect your virtue in great matters;—in raising a mound of nine fathoms, the work may be unfinished for want of one basket (of earth).

LXXI. The Master said: What is required in feeling is sincerity; in words, that they be susceptible of proof.

* * * * *

The superior man, while (his parents) are

alive, reverently nourishes them; and, when they are dead, he reverently sacrifices to them;—his (chief) thought is how to the end of life not to disgrace them.

* * * * *

On the bathing-tub of Thang the following words were engraved: If you can one day renovate yourself, do so from day to day. Yea, daily renovate yourself.

* * * * *

Twitters fast the oriole
   Where yonder bends the mound,
The happy little creature
   Its resting-place has found.

The Master said: Yes, it rests: it knows where to rest. Can one be a man, and yet not equal (in this respect) to this bird?

* * * * *

All the living must die, and dying, return to the ground. . . . The bones and flesh moulder below, and, hidden away, become the earth of the fields. But the spirit issues forth, and is displayed on high in a condition of glorious brightness.

* * * * *

Perfection of nature is characteristic of Heaven. To attain to that perfection belongs to man.

LXXII. I have brought you Law, and subdued for you iniquity. I am not a doer of fraud and iniquity against men. I am not a doer of that which is crooked in place of that which is right. I am not cognizant of iniquity; I am not a doer of evil. I do not force a laboring man to do more than his daily task. . . . I do not calumniate a servant to his master: I do not cause hunger; I do not cause weeping; I am not a murderer; I do not give order to murder privily; I am not guilty of fraud against any one; I am not a falsifier of the measures in the temples. . . . I do not add to the weight of the scale; I do not falsify the indicator of the balance; I do not withhold milk from the mouth of the suckling.

LXXIII. The Almighty God, the self-existent, who made heaven and earth, the waters, the breaths of life, fire, the gods, men, animals, cattle, reptiles, birds, fishes, kings, men, and gods (in accordance with one single thought) (speaketh): . . . I am the maker of heaven and of the earth. I raise its mountains and the creatures which are upon it; I make the waters, and the Mehura comes into being. . . . I am the maker of heaven, and of the mysteries of the two-fold horizon. It is I who have given to all the gods the soul which is within them. When I open my eyes, there is light; when I close them, there is darkness. . . . I make the hours, and the hours come into existence.

. . . . .

I am yesterday, I am to-day, I am to-morrow.

LXXIV. Hail to thee, O Ptah-tanen, great god who concealeth His form, . . . Thou art watching when at rest; the father of all fathers and of all gods. . . . Watcher, who traversest the endless ages of eternity. The heaven was yet uncreated, uncreated was the earth, the water flowed not; Thou hast put together the earth, Thou hast united Thy limbs, Thou hast reckoned Thy members; what Thou hast found apart, Thou hast put into its place; O God, architect of the world, Thou art without a father, begotten by Thine own becoming; Thou art without a mother, being born through repetition of Thyself. Thou drivest away the darkness by the beams of Thine eyes. Thou ascendest into the zenith of heaven, and Thou comest down even as Thou hast risen. When Thou art a dweller in the infernal world, Thy knees are above the earth, and Thine head is in the upper sky. Thou sustainest the substances which Thou hast made. It is by Thine own strength that Thou movest; Thou art raised up by the might of Thine own arms. Thou weighest upon Thyself, kept firm by the mystery which is in Thee. The roaring of Thy voice is in the cloud; Thy breath is on the mountain-tops; the waters of the inundation cover the lofty trees of every region. . . . Heaven and earth obey the commands which Thou hast given; they travel by the road which Thou hast laid down for them; they transgress not the path which Thou hast prescribed to them, and which Thou hast opened to them. . . . Thou restest, and it is night; when Thine eyes shine forth, we are illuminated. . . . O let us give glory to the God who hath raised up the sky, and who causeth His disk to float over the bosom of Nut, who hath made the gods and men and all their generations, who hath made all lands and countries, and the great sea, in His name of " Let-the-earth-be "! . . . The babe who is brought forth daily, the ancient one who has reached the limits of time, the immovable one who traverses every path, the height which cannot be attained.

LXXV. Hail to Thee, Amon Rā, Lord of the thrones of the earth, . . . the ancient of heaven, the oldest of the earth, Lord of all existences, the support of things, the support of all things. The ONE in his works, single among the gods: . . . chief of all the gods; Lord of truth, father of the gods; maker of men, creator of beasts, maker of herbs, feeder of cattle, good power begotten of Ptah, . . . to whom the gods give honor. Maker of things below and above, enlightener of the earth, sailing in heaven in tranquillity; King Rā, triumphant one, chief of the earth. Most glorious one, . . . chief maker of the earth after His image, how great are His thoughts above every god! Hail to Thee, Rā, Lord of law, whose shrine is hidden, Lord of the gods; . . . Atmu, maker of men, . . . giving them life, . . . listening to the poor who is in distress, gentle of heart when one cries to Him. Deliverer of the timid man from the violent, judging the poor, the poor and the oppressed. Lord of wisdom, whose precepts are wise; at whose pleasure the Nile overflows: Lord of mercy, most loving, at whose coming men live: opener of every eye, proceeding from the firmament, causer of pleasure and light;

at whose goodness the gods rejoice; their hearts revive when they see Him. O Rā, adored in Thebes, high-crowned in the house of the obelisk (Heliopolis), sovereign of life, health, and strength, sovereign Lord of all the gods; who art visible in the midst of the horizon, ruler of the past generations and the nether world; whose name is hidden from His creatures. . . .

The ONE, maker of all that is; the One, the only One, the maker of existences; . . . maker of grass for the cattle; of fruitful trees for men of future generations; causing the fish to live in the river, the birds to fill the air; giving breath to those in the egg; feeding the bird that flies; giving food to the bird that perches, to the creeping thing and the flying thing alike; . . . feeding the flying things in every tree.

Hail to Thee for all these things — the *one*, alone with many hands, lying awake while all men sleep, to seek out the good of His creatures, Amon, sustainer of all things: . . . salutation to Thee because Thou abidest in us, adoration to Thee because Thou hast created us.

Hail to Thee, say to all creatures: salutation to Thee from every land; to the height of heaven, to the breadth of the earth, to the depth of the sea: . . . the spirits Thou hast created exalt Thee, rejoicing before the feet of their begetter; they cry out, Welcome to Thee, father of the fathers of all the gods, who raises the heavens, who fixes the earth. Maker of beings, creator of existences, sovereign of life, health, and strength, . . . we worship Thy spirit who alone hast made us; we whom Thou hast made (thank Thee) that Thou hast given us birth; we give Thee praises on account of Thy abiding in us.

Hail to Thee, maker of all beings, Lord of law, father of the gods; maker of men, creator of beasts; Lord of grains, making food for the beast of the field. . . . The ONE alone without a second. . . . King alone, single among the gods; of many names, unknown is their number.

LXXVI. The mysterious names of the god who is *immanent in all things!* . . . He is the body of the living man, the creator of the fruit-bearing tree, the author of the inundation; without Him nothing liveth within the circuit of the earth, whether north or south, under His name of Osiris, the giver of light: He is the Horus of the living souls, the living god of the generations yet to come. He is the creator of every animal. . . . He is the god of those who rest in their graves. Amon is an image, Atmu is an image, Chepera is an image, Rā is an image; He alone maketh Himself in millions of ways. He is a great architect, who was from the beginning, who fashioned His body with His own hands, in all forms according to His will. . . . Permanent and enduring, He never passeth away. Through millions upon millions of endless years He traverseth the heavens, He compasseth the nether world each day. . . . He is the moon in the night and king of the stars, who maketh the division of seasons, months, and years; He cometh living everlastingly both in His rising and in His setting. There is no other like Him; His voice is heard, but He remains unseen to every creature that breathes. He strengthens the heart of the women in travail, and gives life to those who are born from her. . . . He travels in the cloud to separate heaven and earth, and again to reunite them, permanently abiding in all things, the Living One in whom all things live everlastingly.

LXXVII. All that we are is the result of

what we have thought: it is founded on our thoughts, it is made up of our thoughts. If a man speaks or acts with an evil thought, pain follows him, as the wheel follows the foot of the ox that draws the carriage.

All that we are is the result of what we have thought: it is founded on our thoughts, it is made up of our thoughts. If a man speaks or acts with a pure thought, happiness follows him, like a shadow that never leaves him.

"He abused me, he beat me, he defeated me, he robbed me,"—in those who harbor such thoughts hatred will never cease.

"He abused me, he beat me, he defeated me, he robbed me,"—in those who do not harbor such thoughts hatred will cease.

For hatred does not cease by hatred at any time; hatred ceases by love. This is an old rule.

The world does not know that we must all come to an end here;—but those who know it, their quarrels cease at once.

He who lives looking for pleasures only, his senses uncontrolled, immoderate in his food, idle, and weak, Mâra (the tempter) will certainly overthrow him, as the wind throws down a weak tree.

He who lives without looking for pleasures, his senses well controlled, moderate in his food, faithful and strong, him Mâra will certainly not overthrow, any more than the wind throws down a rocky mountain.

He who wishes to put on the yellow dress without having cleansed himself from sin, who disregards also temperance and truth, is unworthy of the yellow dress.

But he who has cleansed himself from sin, is well grounded in all virtues, and regards also temperance and truth, he is indeed worthy of the yellow dress.

As rain breaks through an ill-thatched house, passion will break through an unreflecting mind.

As rain does not break through a well-thatched house, passion will not break through a well-reflecting mind.

The evil-doer suffers in this world, and he suffers in the next: he suffers in both. He suffers when he thinks of the evil he has done: he suffers more when going on the evil path.

The virtuous man is happy in this world, and he is happy in the next; he is happy in both. He is happy when he thinks of the good he has done: he is still more happy when going on the good path.

The thoughtless man, even if he can recite a large portion (of the law), but is not a doer of it, has no share in the priesthood, but is like a cowherd counting the cows of others.

The follower of the law, even if he can recite only a small portion (of the law), but, having forsaken passion and hatred and foolishness, possesses true knowledge and serenity of mind, he, caring for nothing in this world or that to come, has indeed a share in the priesthood.

LXXVIII. As a fletcher makes straight his arrow, a wise man makes straight his trembling and unsteady thought, which is difficult to guard, difficult to hold back.

It is good to tame the mind, which is difficult to hold in and flighty, rushing wherever it listeth; a tamed mind brings happiness.

Let the wise man guard his thoughts, for they are difficult to perceive, very artful, and they rush wherever they list: thoughts well guarded bring happiness.

Those who bridle their mind, which travels far, moves about alone, is without a body, and hides in the chamber (of the heart), will be free from the bonds of Mâra (the tempter).

If a man's thoughts are unsteady, if he does not know the true law, if his peace of mind is troubled, his knowledge will never be perfect.

If a man's thoughts are not dissipated, if his mind is not perplexed, if he has ceased to think of good or evil, then there is no fear for him while he is watchful.

Knowing that this body is (fragile) like a jar, and making this thought firm like a fortress, one should attack Mâra (the tempter) with the weapon of knowledge, one should watch him when conquered, and should never rest.

Whatever a hater may do to a hater, or an enemy to an enemy, a wrongly directed mind will do us greater mischief.

Not a mother, not a father will do so much, nor any other relative; a well-directed mind will do us greater service.

LXXIX. If a man would hasten toward the good, he should keep his thought away from evil; if a man does what is good slothfully, his mind delights in evil.

Even an evil-doer sees happiness as long as his evil deed has not ripened; but when his evil deed has ripened, then does the evil-doer see evil.

Even a good man sees evil days, as long as his good deed has not ripened; but when his good deed has ripened, then does the good man see happy days.

Let no man think lightly of evil, saying in his heart, It will not come nigh unto me. Even by the falling of water-drops a water-pot is filled; the fool becomes full of evil, even if he gather it little by little.

Let no man think lightly of good, saying in his heart, It will not come nigh unto me. Even by the falling of water-drops a water-pot is filled; the wise man becomes full of good, even if he gather it little by little.

Let a man avoid evil deeds, as a merchant, if he has few companions and carries much wealth, avoids a dangerous road; as a man who loves life avoids poison.

Some people are born again; evil-doers go to hell; righteous people go to heaven; those who are free from all worldly desires attain Nirvâna.

Not in the sky, not in the midst of the sea, not if we enter into the clefts of the mountains, is there known a spot in the whole world where a man might be freed from an evil deed.

Not in the sky, not in the midst of the sea, not if we enter into the clefts of the mountains, is there known a spot in the whole world where death could not overcome (the mortal).

LXXX. Do not follow the evil law! Do not live on in thoughtlessness! Do not follow false doctrine! Be not a friend of the world.

Rouse thyself! do not be idle! Follow the law of virtue! The virtuous rests in bliss in this world and in the next.

Look upon the world as a bubble, look upon it as a mirage; the king of death does not see him who thus looks down upon the world.

Come, look at this glittering world, like unto a royal chariot; the foolish are immersed in it, but the wise do not touch it.

He who formerly was reckless and afterwards became sober brightens up this world, like the moon when freed from clouds.

This world is dark, few only can see here; a few only go to heaven, like birds escaped from the net.

Better than sovereignty over the earth, better than going to heaven, better than lordship over all worlds, is the reward of the first step in holiness.

LXXXI. He whose conquest is not conquered again, into whose conquest no one in this world enters, by what track can you lead him, the Awakened, the Omniscient, the trackless?

He whom no desire with its snares and poisons can lead astray, by what track can you lead him, the Awakened, the Omniscient, the trackless?

Even the gods envy those who are awakened and not forgetful, who are given to meditation, who are wise, and who delight in the repose of retirement (from the world).

Difficult (to obtain) is the conception of men, difficult is the life of mortals, difficult is the hearing of the True Law, difficult is the birth of the Awakened (the attainment of Buddhahood).

Not to commit any sin, to do good, and to purify one's mind, that is the teaching of (all) the Awakened.

Not to blame, not to strike, to live restrained under the law, to be moderate in eating, to sleep and sit alone, and to dwell on the highest thoughts,—this is the teaching of the Awakened.

There is no satisfying lusts, even by a shower of gold pieces; he who knows that lusts have a short taste and cause pain, he is wise.

Men, driven by fear, go to many a refuge, to mountains and forests, to groves and sacred trees.

But that is not a safe refuge, that is not the best refuge; a man is not delivered from all pains after having gone to that refuge.

He who takes refuge with Buddha, the Law, and the Church; he who, with clear understanding, sees the four holy truths:—

Viz.: pain, the origin of pain, the destruction of pain, and the eight-fold holy way that leads to the quieting of pain;—

That is the safe refuge, that is the best refuge; having gone to that refuge, a man is delivered from all pain.

Happy is the arising of the awakened, happy is the teaching of the True Law, happy is peace in the church, happy is the devotion of those who are at peace.

LXXXII. Let a man leave anger, let him forsake pride, let him overcome all bondage! No sufferings befall the man who is not attached to name and form, and who calls nothing his own.

He who holds back rising anger like a rolling chariot, him I call a real driver; other people are but holding the reins.

Let a man overcome anger by love, let him overcome evil by good; let him overcome the greedy by liberality, the liar by truth!

Speak the truth, do not yield to anger; give, if thou art asked for little; by these three steps thou wilt go near the gods.

Beware of bodily anger, and control thy body! Leave the sins of the body, and with thy body practise virtue!

Beware of the anger of the tongue, and control thy tongue! Leave the sins of the tongue and practise virtue with thy tongue!

Beware of the anger of the mind, and control thy mind! Leave the sins of the mind, and practise virtue with thy mind!

The wise who control their body, who control their tongue, the wise who control their mind, are indeed well controlled.

LXXXIII. All created things perish; he

who knows and sees this becomes passive in pain; this is the way to purity.

All forms are unreal; he who knows and sees this becomes passive in pain; this is the way that leads to purity.

Watching his speech, well restrained in mind, let a man never commit any wrong with his body! Let a man but keep these three roads of action clear, and he will achieve the way which is taught by the wise.

Cut down the whole forest (of lust), not a tree only! Danger comes out of the forest (of lust). When you have cut down both the forest (of lust) and its undergrowth, then, Bhikshus, you will be rid of the forest and free!

Cut out the love of self, like an autumn lotus, with thy hand! Cherish the road of peace. Nirvâna has been shown by Sugata (Buddha).

A wise and good man who knows the meaning of this should quickly clear the way that leads to Nirvâna.

LXXXIV. He who is thoughtful, blameless, settled, dutiful, without passions, and who has attained the highest end, him I call indeed a Brâhmana.

Him I call indeed a Brâhmana who does not offend by body, word, or thought, and is controlled on these three points.

A man does not become a Brâhmana by his platted hair, by his family, or by birth; in whom there is truth and righteousness, he is blessed, he is a Brâhmana.
What is the use of platted hair, O fool! what of the raiment of goat-skins? Within thee there is ravening, but the outside thou makest clean.

Him I call indeed a Brâhmana who has cut all fetters, who never troubles, is independent and unshackled.

Him I call indeed a Brâhmana who, though he has committed no offence, endures reproach, bonds, and stripes, who has endurance for his force and strength for his army.
Him I call indeed a Brâhmana who is free from anger, dutiful, virtuous, without appetite, who is subdued, and has received his last body.

Him I call indeed a Brâhmana who does not cling to pleasures, like water on a lotus leaf, like a mustard seed on the point of a needle.

Him I call indeed a Brâhmana whose knowledge is deep, who possesses wisdom, who knows the right way and the wrong, and has attained the highest end.

Him I call indeed a Brâhmana who finds no fault with other beings, whether feeble or strong, and does not kill nor cause slaughter.

Him I call indeed a Brâhmana who is tolerant with the intolerant, mild with fault-finders, and free from passion among the passionate.

Him I call indeed a Brâhmana from whom anger and hatred, pride and envy have dropped like a mustard seed from the point of a needle.

Him I call indeed a Brâhmana who utters true speech, instructive and free from harshness, so that he offend no one.

Him I call indeed a Brâhmana who calls nothing his own, whether it be before, behind, or between, who is poor, and free from the love of the world.

Him I call indeed a Brâhmana, the manly, the noble, the hero, the great sage, the conqueror, the impassible, the accomplished, the awakened.

LXXXV. The inhabitants that dwell in the Blessed One's City of Righteousness, O King, are such as these:

Men devoid of passion, and of malice, and of dulness, men in whom the Great Evils (lust, becoming, delusion, and ignorance) are not, men who have neither craving thirst, nor grasping desires—those are they who dwell in the City of Righteousness.

The earnest and prudent, heroes who feed on little and know no greed, content whether they receive an alms or receive it not—these are they who dwell in the City of Righteousness.

The meditative, delighting in Ghâna, heroes of tranquil minds and steadfast, looking forward to Nirvâna—these are they who dwell in the City of Righteousness.

Men walking in the path, and standing in the fruits thereof, those who have attained some fruits thereof but are yet learners as to the last, whose hope is directed to the utmost goal—these are they who dwell in the City of Righteousness.

Those skilled in the means of attaining undisturbed self-possession, and rejoicing in contemplation on the seven-fold wisdom, those who are full of insight, and bear the words of the Dhamma in their hearts—these are they who dwell in the City of Righteousness.

Those of downcast eyes and measured speech, the doors of whose senses are guarded, who are self-restrained, who are well trained according to the supreme Dhamma—these are they who dwell in the City of Righteousness.

And furthermore, O King, those of the Bhikkhus who are pure and stainless, in whom no evil dispositions are left, who, skilful in the knowledge of the fall and rise of beings, have perfected themselves in the Divine Eye—such Bhikkhus are called, O King, "The givers of light in the Blessed One's City of Righteousness."

And furthermore, O King, those of the Bhikkhus who wear on their brows the lotus garland of that noble Emancipation, who have attained to that highest and best and most exceeding excellent of all conditions, who are loved and longed for by the great multitudes — such Bhikkhus are called, O King, "Flower-sellers in the Blessed One's City of Righteousness."

And furthermore, O King, those of the Bhikkhus who, being anointed with that most excellent perfume of right conduct, are gifted with many and various virtues, and are able to dispel the bad odor of sin and evil dispositions—such Bhikkhus are called, O King, "Perfume dealers in the Blessed One's City of Righteousness."

And furthermore, O King, those of the Bhikkhus who in the spirit and in the letter, in its arguments and explanations, in its reasons and examples, teach and repeat, utter forth and recapitulate the nine-fold word of the Buddha — such Bhikkhus are called, O King, "Lawyers (dealers in Dhamma) in the Blessed One's City of Righteousness."

And furthermore, O King, those of the Bhikkhus who have penetrated to the sublimer teaching, who understand exposition and the divisions of objects of meditation to be practised, who are perfect in all the subtler points of training — such Bhikkhus are called, O King, "Distinguished masters of law in the Blessed One's City of Righteousness."

Thus well planned out, O King, is the Blessed One's City of Righteousness, thus well built, thus well appointed, thus well provisioned, thus well established, thus well guarded, thus well protected, thus impregnable by enemies or foes. And by this explanation, O King, by this argument, by this reason, you may by inference know that the Blessed One did once exist.

## LXXXVI.

As when they see a pleasant city, well planned out,
Men know, by inference, how great the founder was;
So when they see our Lord's "City of Righteousness"
They know, by inference, that he did once exist.

As men, seeing its waves, can judge, by inference,
The great extent and power of the world-embracing sea;

So may they judge the Buddha when they see the waves
That he set rolling through the world of gods and men—
He who, unconquered in the fight, allays all griefs,
Who rooted out, in his own heart, Craving's dread power,
And set his followers free from the whirlpool of rebirths—
" Far as the waves of the Good-Law extend and roll,
So great, so mighty, must our Lord, the Buddha, be."


As men, seeing its mighty peaks that tower aloft,
Can judge, by inference, Himâlaya's wondrous height;
So when they see the Buddha's Mount of Righteousness—
Steadfast, unshaken by fierce passion's stormy blasts,
Towering aloft in wondrous heights of calm and peace,
Where lusts, evil, and Karma cannot breathe or live,—

They draw the inference: "Great as this mountain high
That mighty Hero's power upon whose word it stands."

   .    .    .    .    .

Seeing the earth smiling, well watered, green with grass,
Men say: "A great and pleasant rain hath fallen fast."
So when they see this multitude rejoicing, peaceful, blest,
Men may infer: "How sweet the rain that stilled their hearts!"

   .    .    .    .    .

As when men, travelling, feel a glorious perfume sweet
Pervading all the country side, and gladdening them, infer at once,
"Surely, 't is giant forest trees are flowering now!"
So, conscious of this perfume sweet of righteousness
That now pervades the earth and heavens, they may infer:
"A Buddha, infinitely great, must once have lived!"

LXXXVII. Reverence to the Blessed One, the Holy One, the Fully Enlightened One.

Thus have I heard: The Blessed One was once staying at Benares, at the hermitage called Migadâya. And there the Blessed One addressed the company of the five Bhikkhus, and said:

"There are two extremes, O Bhikkhus, which the man who has given up the world ought not to follow—the habitual practice, on the one hand, of those things whose attraction depends upon the passions, and especially of sensuality—a low and pagan way (of seeking satisfaction), unworthy, unprofitable, and fit only for the worldly minded—and the habitual practice, on the other hand, of asceticism (or self-mortification), which is painful, unworthy, and unprofitable.

"There is a middle path, O Bhikkhus, avoiding the two extremes, discovered by the Tathâgata—a path which opens the eyes, and bestows understanding, which leads to peace of mind, to the higher wisdom, to full enlightenment, to Nirvâna!

"What is that middle path, O Bhikkhus, avoiding these two extremes, discovered by the Tathâgata—that path which opens the eyes, and bestows understanding, which leads to peace of mind, to the higher wisdom, to full enlightenment, to Nirvâna?

Verily! it is this noble eight-fold path; that is to say:

> "Right views;
> Right aspirations;
> Right speech;
> Right conduct;
> Right livelihood;
> Right effort;
> Right mindfulness; and
> Right contemplation.

"This, O Bhikkhus, is that middle path, avoiding these two extremes, discovered by the Tathâgata — that path which opens the eyes, and bestows understanding, which leads to peace of mind, to the higher wisdom, to full enlightenment, to Nirvâna!"

LXXXVIII. Putting away the murder of that which lives, he abstains from destroying life. The cudgel and the sword he lays aside; and, full of modesty and pity, he is compassionate and kind to all creatures that have life!

Putting away the theft of that which is not his, he abstains from taking anything not given. He takes only what is given; therewith is he content, and he passes his life in honesty and in purity of heart!

Putting away unchastity, he lives a life of chastity and purity!

Putting away lying, he abstains from speaking falsehood. He speaks truth, from the truth he never swerves; faithful and trustworthy, he injures not his fellowman by deceit.

Putting away slander, he abstains from calumny. What he hears here he repeats not elsewhere to raise a quarrel against the people here: what he hears elsewhere he repeats not here to raise a quarrel against the people there. Thus he lives as a binder together of those who are divided, an encourager of those who are friends, a peacemaker, a lover of peace, impassioned for peace, a speaker of words that make for peace.

Putting away bitterness of speech, he abstains from harsh language. Whatever word is humane, pleasant to the ear, lovely, reaching to the heart, urbane, pleasing to the people, beloved of the people — such are the words he speaks.

Putting away foolish talk, he abstains from vain conversation. In season he speaks; he speaks that which is; he speaks fact; he utters good doctrine; he utters good discipline; he speaks, and at the right time, that which redounds to profit, is well grounded, is well defined, and is full of wisdom.

. . . . .

This is the kind of goodness that he has.

LXXXIX. O Thou who hast many names, but whose power is infinite and uncommunicated! O Jupiter, first of immortals, sovereign of nature, who governest all, who subjectest all to Thy law, I worship Thee; for man is permitted to invoke Thee. Everything that lives or creeps, everything mortal on earth is from Thee, and of Thee but an imperfect image. I will address to Thee my hymns, and will never cease to celebrate Thee.

This universe expanded over our heads, and which seems to roll around the earth, is obedient to Thee alone; and at Thy command are its motions in silence performed. Thunder, the executioner of Thy will, is launched by Thy invincible arm. Endowed with immortal life, it strikes, and nature is appalled.

Thou directest the universal mind that animates the whole, and that exists in all Thy creatures; so unlimited and supreme is Thy power, O King! Nothing in heaven, on the earth, or in the sea is produced without Thee, except the evil that proceeds from the heart of the wicked.

Thou bringest order out of confusion, and by Thee is the jarring of the elements composed. Thou hast so mingled good and evil that general and universal harmony is established. The wicked alone, amongst all Thy creatures, disturb this general harmony.

Wretched men! they seek for happiness, but do not comprehend Thy universal law that by making them wise would make them good, and consequently happy; but declining from the path of what is beautiful and just, they run headlong to the object that attracts them; they pant after fame, they grasp at sordid treasures, they lust after pleasures that entice but to deceive them.

O God! from whom all blessings descend, whom the storm and the thunder obey, preserve us from error; deign to inform our minds; attach us to that eternal reason by which Thou art guided and supported in the government of the world; that being ourselves honored we may also honor Thee, as becomes feeble and mortal beings, by celebrating Thy works in an uninterrupted hymn;

for neither the inhabitant of earth, nor the inhabitant of heaven can be engaged in a service more noble than that of celebrating the divine mind which presides over Nature. *Amen.*

XC. I went to one man after another, being not unconscious of the enmity which I provoked, and I lamented and feared this: but necessity was laid upon me,—the word of God, I thought, ought to be considered first. And I said to myself, Go I must to all who appear to know, and find out the meaning of the oracle.

I am called wise, for my hearers always imagine that I myself possess the wisdom which I find wanting in others: but the truth is, O men of Athens, that God only is wise; and in His answer He means to say that the wisdom of men is little or nothing; He is not speaking of Socrates, He is only using my name by way of illustration, as if He said, He, O men, is the wisest, who, like Socrates, knows that his wisdom is in truth worth nothing.

Some one will say: And are you not ashamed, Socrates, of a course of life which is likely to bring you to an untimely end? To him I may fairly answer: There you are mistaken: a man who is good for anything ought not to calculate the chance of living or dying; he ought only to consider whether in doing anything he is doing right or wrong—acting the part of a good man or of a bad.

. . . . .

For wherever a man's place is, whether the place which he has chosen or that in which he has been placed by a commander, there he ought to remain in the hour of danger; he should not think of death or of anything but of disgrace. And this, O men of Athens, is a true saying.

If, I say, now, when, as I conceive and imagine, God orders me to fulfil the philosopher's mission of searching into myself and other men, I were to desert my post through fear of death, or any other fear; that would indeed be strange, and I might justly be arraigned in court for denying the existence of the gods, if I disobeyed the oracle because I was afraid of death: then I should be fancying that I was wise when I was not wise.

. . . . .

Men of Athens, I honor and love you; but

I shall obey God rather than you, and while I have life and strength I shall never cease from the practice and teaching of philosophy, exhorting any one whom I meet after my manner, and convincing him, saying: O my friend, why do you, who are a citizen of the great and mighty and wise city of Athens, care so much about laying up the greatest amount of money and honor and reputation, and so little about wisdom and truth and the greatest improvement of the soul, which you never regard or heed at all?

I do nothing but go about persuading you all, old and young alike, not to take thought for your persons or your properties, but first and chiefly to care about the greatest improvement of the soul.

Some one will say: Yes, Socrates, but cannot you hold your tongue, and then you may go into a foreign city, and no one will interfere with you? Now I have great difficulty in making you understand my answer to this. For if I tell you that to do as you say would be a disobedience to the God, and therefore that I cannot hold my tongue, you will not believe that I am serious; and if I say again that the greatest good of man is daily to converse about virtue, and all that concerning which you hear me examining myself and others, and that the life which is unexamined is not worth living, you are still less likely to believe me.

The difficulty, my friends, is not in avoiding death, but in avoiding unrighteousness; for that runs faster than death.

XCI. O my judges—for you I may truly call judges—I should like to tell you of a wonderful circumstance. Hitherto the familiar oracle within me has constantly been in the habit of opposing me even about trifles, if I were going to make a slip or error in any matter; and now, as you see, there has come upon me that which may be thought, and is generally believed to be, the last and worst evil. But the oracle made no sign of opposition, either as I was leaving my house and going out in the morning, or when I was going up into this court, or while I was speaking, at anything which I was going to say; and yet I have often been stopped in the middle of a speech, but now in nothing I either said or did touching this matter has the oracle opposed me. What do I take to be the explanation of this? I will tell you. I regard this as a great proof that what has happened to me is a good, and that those of us who think that death is an evil are in error. For the customary sign would surely have opposed me had I been going to evil and not to good.

Let us reflect in another way, and we shall see that there is great reason to hope that death is a good; for one of two things—either death is a state of nothingness and utter unconsciousness, or, as men say, there is a change and migration of the soul from this world to another. Now if you suppose that there is no consciousness, but a sleep like the sleep of him who is undisturbed even by the sight of dreams, death will be an unspeakable gain. For if a person were to select the night in which his sleep was undisturbed even by dreams, and were to compare with this the other days and nights of his life, and then were to tell us how many days and nights he had passed in the course of his life better and more pleasantly than this one, I think that any man, I will not say a private man, but even the great king will not find many such days or nights, when compared with the

others. Now if death is like this, I say that
to die is gain; for eternity is then only a
single night. But if death is the journey to
another place, and there, as men say, all the
dead are, what good, O my friends and
judges, can be greater than this? If indeed
when the pilgrim arrives in the world below,
he is delivered from the professors of justice
in this world, and finds the true judges who
are said to give judgment there, Minos and
Rhadamanthus and Æacus and Triptolemus,
and other sons of God who were righteous in
their own life, that pilgrimage will be worth
making. What would not a man give if he
might converse with Orpheus and Musæus
and Hesiod and Homer? Nay, if this be
true, let me die again and again. I myself,
too, shall have a wonderful interest in there
meeting and conversing with Palamedes, and
Ajax the son of Telamon, and other heroes
of old, who have suffered death through an
unjust judgment; and there will be no small
pleasure, as I think, in comparing my own
sufferings with theirs. Above all, I shall
then be able to continue my search into true
and false knowledge; as in this world, so
also in that; and I shall find out who is wise,
and who pretends to be wise, and is not.

. . . What infinite delight would there be in conversing with them and asking them questions! In another world they do not put a man to death for asking questions; assuredly not. For besides being happier in that world than in this, they will be immortal, if what is said is true.

Wherefore, O judges, be of good cheer about death, and know of a certainty that no evil can happen to a good man, either in life or after death. He and his are not neglected by the gods; nor has my own approaching end happened by mere chance. But I see clearly that to die and be released was better for me; and therefore the oracle gave no sign. For which reason, also, I am not angry with my condemners, or with my accusers; they have done me no harm, although they did not mean to do me any good; and for this I may gently blame them.

The hour of departure has arrived, and we go our ways — I to die, and you to live. Which is better God only knows.

XCII. In all parts of the earth there are hollows of various forms and sizes, into which the water and the mist and the lower air collect; and the true earth is pure and in the pure heaven, in which also are the stars—that is the heaven which is commonly spoken of as the ether, of which this is but the sediment gathering in the hollows of the earth. But we who live in these hollows are deceived into the notion that we are dwelling above on the surface of the earth; which is just as if a creature who was at the bottom of the sea were to fancy that he was on the surface of the water, and that the sea was the heaven through which he saw the sun and the other stars — he having never come to the surface by reason of his feebleness and sluggishness, and having never lifted up his head and seen, nor ever heard from one who had seen, how much purer and fairer the world above is than his own. And such is exactly our case: for we are dwelling in a hollow of the earth, and fancy that we are on the surface; and the air we call the heaven, wherein we imagine that the stars move. But this again is owing to our feebleness and sluggishness, which prevent our reaching the surface of the air: for if any man could arrive at the exterior limit, or take the wings of a bird and fly upward, then like a fish who puts his head out and sees this world, he would see a world beyond; and, if the nature of man could sustain the sight, he would acknowledge that this other world was the place of the true heaven and the true light and the true earth. For our earth, and the stones, and the entire region which surrounds us, are spoilt and corroded, as in the sea all things are corroded by the brine, and there is hardly any noble or perfect growth, but clefts only, and sand, and an endless slough of mud; and even the shore is not to be compared to the fairer sights of this world. And still less is this our world to be compared with the other.

. . . . .

XCIII. There the whole earth is made up of them (various colors), and they are brighter far and clearer than ours; there is a purple of wonderful lustre, also the radiance of gold, and the white which is in the earth whiter than any chalk or snow. Of these and other colors the earth is made up, and they are more in number and fairer than the eye of man has ever seen; and the very hollows (of which I was speaking) filled with air and water have a color of their own, and are seen like light gleaming amid the diversity of the other colors, so that the whole presents an appearance of variety in unity. And in this fair region everything that grows—trees, and flowers, and fruits—are in a like degree fairer than any here; and there are hills, and stones in them in a like degree smoother, and more transparent, and fairer in color than our highly valued emeralds and sardonyxes and jaspers, and other gems, which are but minute fragments of them: for there all the stones are like our precious stones, and fairer still. The reason of this is, that they are pure, and not, like our precious stones, infected or corroded by the corrupt briny elements which coagulate among us, and which breed foulness and disease both in earth and stones, as well as in animals and plants. They are the jewels of the upper earth, which also shines with gold and silver and the like, and they are set in the light of day and are large and abundant and in all places, making the earth a sight to gladden the beholder's eye. And there are animals and men, some in a middle region, others dwelling about the air as we dwell about the sea; others in islands which the air flows round, near the continent: and in a word, the air is used by them as the water and the sea are by us, and the ether is to them what the air is to us. Moreover, the temperament of their season is such that they have no disease, and live much longer than we do, and have sight and hearing and smell, and all the other senses, in far greater perfection, in the same degree that air is purer than water or the ether than air. Also they have temples and sacred places in which the gods really dwell, and they hear their voices and receive their answers, and are conscious of them and hold converse with them, and they see the sun, moon, and stars as they really are, and their other blessedness is of a piece with this.

XCIV. Such is the nature of the other world; and when the dead arrive at the place to which the genius of each severally conveys them, first of all, they have sentence passed upon them, as they have lived well and piously or not. And those who appear to have lived neither well nor ill go to the river Acheron, and using such means of conveyance as they have, are carried in them to the lake, and there they dwell and are purified of their evil deeds, and suffer the penalty of the wrongs which they have done to others, and are absolved, and receive the rewards of their good deeds according to their deserts. But those who appear to be incurable by reason of the greatness of their crimes—who have committed many and terrible deeds of sacrilege, murders foul and violent, or the like—such are hurled into Tartarus, which is their suitable destiny, and they never come out. Those again who have committed crimes, which, although great, are not irremediable—who in a moment of anger, for example, have done some violence to a father or a mother, and have repented for the remainder of their lives, or who have taken the life of another under the like extenuating circumstances—these are plunged into Tartarus, the pains of which they are compelled to undergo for a year, but at the end of the year the wave casts them forth — mere homicides by way of Cocytus, parricides and matricides by Pyriphlegethon—and they are borne to the Acherusian lake, and there they lift up their voices and call upon the victims whom they have slain or wronged to have pity on them, and to be kind to them, and let them come out into the lake. And if they prevail, then they come forth and cease from their troubles; but if not, they are carried back again into Tartarus and from thence into the rivers unceasingly, until they obtain mercy from those whom they have wronged: for that is the sentence inflicted upon them by their judges.

Those, too, who have been pre-eminent for holiness of life are released from this earthly prison, and go to their pure home which is above, and dwell in the purer earth; and those who have duly purified themselves with philosophy live henceforth altogether without the body, in mansions fairer far than these, which may not be described, and of which the time would fail me to tell.

Wherefore, . . . seeing all these things, what ought not we to do that we may obtain virtue and wisdom in this life? Fair is the prize, and the hope great!

XCV. He who has been instructed thus far in the things of love, and who has learned to see the beautiful in due order and succession, when he comes toward the end will suddenly perceive a nature of wondrous beauty (and this, Socrates, is the final cause of all our former toils)—a nature which in the first place is everlasting, not growing and decaying, or waxing and waning; in the next place not fair in one point of view and foul in another, or at one time or in one relation or at one place fair, at another time or in another relation or at another place foul, as if fair to some and foul to others, or in the likeness of a face or hands or any other part of the bodily frame, or in any form of speech or knowledge, or existing in any other being; as, for example, in an animal, or in heaven, or in earth, or in any other place, but beauty only, absolute, separate, simple, and everlasting, which without diminution and without increase, or any change, is imparted to the ever-growing and perishing beauties of all other things. He who under the influence of true love rising upward from these begins to see that beauty is not far from the end. And the true order of going or being led by another to the things of love is to use the beauties of earth as steps along which he mounts upwards for the sake of that other beauty, going from one to two, and from two to all fair forms, and from fair forms to fair practices, and from fair practices to fair notions, until from fair notions he arrives at the notion of absolute beauty, and at last knows what the essence of beauty is. . . . But what if man had eyes to see the true beauty—the divine beauty, I mean, pure and clear and unalloyed, not clogged with the pollutions of mortality, and all the colors and vanities of human life — thither looking, and holding converse with the true beauty divine and simple? Do you not see that in that communion only, beholding beauty with the eye of the mind, he will be enabled to bring forth, not images of beauty, but realities (for he has hold not of an image but of a reality), and bringing forth and nourishing true virtue to become the friend of God and be immortal, if mortal man may. Would that be an ignoble life?

XCVI. There is a victory and defeat—the first and best of victories, the lowest and worst of defeats—which each man gains or sustains at the hands, not of another, but of himself.

The goods of which the many speak are not really good: first in the catalogue is placed health, beauty next, wealth third; and then innumerable others. . . . While to the just and holy all these things are the best of possessions, to the unjust they are all, including even health, the greatest of evils.

The life which is by the Gods deemed to be the happiest is the holiest.

He who thinks that he can honor the soul by word or gift, or any sort of compliance, without making her in any way better, seems to honor her, but honors her not at all.

When any one prefers beauty to virtue, what is this but the real and utter dishonor of the soul?

All the gold which is under or upon the earth is not enough to give in exchange for virtue.

No one, as I may say, ever considers that which is declared to be the greatest penalty of evil-doing—namely, to grow into the likeness of bad men, and growing like them to fly from the conversation of the good, and be cut off from them, and cleave to and follow after the company of the bad.

He who would be dear to God must, as far as is possible, be like Him and such as He is.

XCVII. Every moment think steadily as a Roman and a man to do what thou hast in hand with perfect and simple dignity, and feeling of affection, and freedom, and justice; and to give thyself relief from all other thoughts. And thou wilt give thyself relief, if thou doest every act of thy life as if it were the last, laying aside all carelessness and passionate aversion from the commands of reason, and all hypocrisy, and self-love, and discontent with the portion which has been given thee.

Since it is possible that thou mayest depart from life this very moment, regulate every act and thought accordingly. But to go away from among men, if there are gods, is not a thing to be afraid of, for the gods will not involve thee in evil; but if indeed they do not exist, or if they have no concern about human affairs, what is it to me to live in a universe devoid of gods or devoid of providence? But in truth they do exist, and they do care for human things, and they have put all the means in man's power to enable him not to fall into real evils.

Nothing is more wretched than a man who traverses everything in a round, and pries into the things beneath the earth, as the poet says, and seeks by conjecture what is in the minds of his neighbors, without perceiving that it is sufficient to attend to the dæmon within him, and to reverence it sincerely.

And reverence of the dæmon consists in keeping it pure from passion and thoughtlessness, and dissatisfaction with what comes from gods and men.

For the man who no longer delays being among the number of the best, is like a priest and minister of the gods, using too the (deity) which is planted within him, which makes the man uncontaminated by pleasure, unharmed by any pain, untouched by any insult, feeling no wrong, a fighter in the noblest fight, one who cannot be overpowered by any passion, dyed deep with justice, accepting with all his soul everything which happens and is assigned to him as his portion.

XCVIII. If thou findest in human life anything better than justice, truth, temperance, fortitude, and, in a word, anything better than thine own mind's self-satisfaction in the things which it enables thee to do according to right reason, and in the condition that is assigned to thee without thine own choice: if, I say, thou seest anything better than this, turn to it with all thy soul, and enjoy that which thou hast found to be the best. But if nothing appears to be better than the deity which is planted in thee, which has subjected to itself all thine appetites, and carefully examines all the impressions, and, as Socrates said, has detached itself from the persuasions of sense, and has submitted itself to the gods, and cares for mankind; if thou findest everything else smaller and of less value than this, give place to nothing else, for if thou dost once diverge and incline to it, thou wilt no longer without distraction be able to give the preference to that good thing which is thy proper possession and thine own; for it is not right that anything of any other kind, such as praise from the many, or power, or enjoyment of pleasure, should come into competition with that which is rationally and politically (or, practically) good.

Never value anything as profitable to thyself which shall compel thee to break thy promise, to lose thy self-respect, to hate any man, to suspect, to curse, to act the hypocrite, to desire anything which needs walls and curtains: for he who has preferred to everything else his own intelligence and dæmon and the worship of its excellence acts no tragic part, does not groan, will not need either solitude or much company; and, what is chief of all, he will live without either pursuing or flying from (death); but whether for a longer or a shorter time he shall have the soul inclosed in the body, he cares not at all: for even if he must depart immediately, he will go as readily as if he were going to do anything else which can be done with decency and order; taking care of this only all through life, that his thoughts turn not away from anything which belongs to an intelligent animal and a member of a civil community.

XCIX. Everything harmonizes with me, which is harmonious to thee, O Universe. Nothing for me is too early nor too late which is in due time for thee. Everything is fruit to me which thy seasons bring, O Nature: from thee are all things, in thee are all things, to thee all things return. The poet says, Dear city of Cecrops; and will not thou say, Dear city of Zeus?

Constantly regard the universe as one living being, having one substance and one soul; and observe how all things have reference to one perception, the perception of this one living being; and how all things act with one movement; and how all things are the cooperating causes of all things which exist; observe too the continuous spinning of the thread and the contexture of the web.

Such as are thy habitual thoughts, such also will be the character of thy mind; for the soul is dyed by the thoughts. Dye it then with a continuous series of such thoughts as these: for instance, that where a man can live, there he can also live well. But he must live in a palace;—well, then, he can also live well in a palace.

Reverence that which is best in the universe; and this is that which makes use of all things, and directs all things. And in like manner also reverence that which is best in thyself; and this is of the same kind as that. For in thyself, also, that which makes use of everything else is this, and thy life is directed by this.

Live with the gods. And he does live with the gods who constantly shows to them that his own soul is satisfied with that which is assigned to him, and that it does all that the dæmon wishes, which Zeus hath given to every man for his guardian and guide, a portion of himself. And this is every man's understanding and reason.

C. Let it make no difference to thee whether thou art cold or warm, if thou art doing thy duty; and whether thou art drowsy or satisfied with sleep; and whether ill spoken of or praised; and whether dying or doing something else. For it is one of the acts of life, this act by which we die: it is sufficient, then, in this act also to do well what we have in hand.

The universe is either a confusion, and a mutual involution of things, and a dispersion; or it is unity and order and providence. If, then, it be the former, why do I desire to tarry in a fortuitous combination of things and such a disorder? and why do I care about anything else than how I shall at last become earth? and why am I disturbed, for the dispersion of my elements will happen whatever I do. But if the other supposition be true, I venerate, and I am firm, and I trust in Him who governs.

If a thing is difficult to be accomplished by thyself, do not think that it is impossible for man: but if anything is possible for man and conformable to his nature, think that this can be attained by thyself too.

Remember the constancy of the Emperor

Antoninus in every act which was conformable to reason, and his evenness in all things, and his piety, and the serenity of his countenance, and his sweetness, and his disregard of empty fame, and his efforts to understand things; and how he would never let anything pass without having first most carefully examined it and clearly understood it; and how he bore with those who blamed him unjustly without blaming them in return; how he did nothing in a hurry; and how he listened not to calumnies, and how exact an examiner of manners and actions he was; and not given to reproach people, nor timid, nor suspicious, nor a sophist; and with how little he was satisfied, such as lodging, bed, dress, food, servants; and how laborious and patient; . . . and his firmness and uniformity in his friendships; and how he tolerated freedom of speech in those who opposed his opinions; and the pleasure that he had when any man showed him anything better; and how religious he was without superstition. Imitate all this that thou mayest have as good a conscience, when thy last hour comes, as he had.

CI. My city and country, so far as I am

Antoninus, is Rome, but so far as I am a man, it is the world. The things, then, which are useful to these cities are alone useful to me.

Every man is worth just so much as the things are worth about which he busies himself.

All things are implicated with one another, and the bond is holy; and there is hardly anything unconnected with any other thing. For things have been co-ordinated, and they combine to form the same universe (order). For there is one universe made up of all things, and one god who pervades all things, and one substance, and one law, (one) common reason in all intelligent animals, and one truth.

Retire into thyself. The rational principle which rules has this nature, that it is content with itself when it does what is just, and so secures tranquillity.

Love mankind. Follow God. The poet says that law rules all. And it is enough to remember that law rules all.

CII. Look within. Within is the fountain of good, and it will ever bubble up, if thou wilt ever dig.

He who acts unjustly acts impiously. For since the universal nature has made rational animals for the sake of one another, to help one another according to their deserts, but in no way to injure one another, he who transgresses her will is clearly guilty of impiety towards the highest divinity. And he too who lies is guilty of impiety to the same divinity; for the universal nature is the nature of things that are; and things that are have a relation to all things that come into existence. And further, this universal nature is named truth, and is the prime cause of all things that are true.

Either there is a fatal necessity and invincible order, or a kind providence, or a confusion without a purpose and without a director. If, then, there is an invincible necessity, why dost thou resist? But if there is a providence which allows itself to be propitiated, make thyself worthy of the help of the divinity. But if there is a confusion without a governor, be content that in such a tempest thou hast in thyself a certain ruling intelligence. And even if the tempest carry thee away, let it carry away the poor flesh, the poor breath, everything else; for the intelligence at least it will not carry away.

Come quick, O death, lest perchance I, too, should forget myself.

CIII. If a man should be able to assent to this doctrine as he ought, that we are all sprung from God in an especial manner, and that God is the Father both of men and of gods, I suppose that he would never have any ignoble or mean thoughts about himself. But if Cæsar (the Emperor) should adopt you, no one could endure your arrogance; and if you know that you are the son of Zeus, will you not be elated? Yet we do not so; but since these two things are mingled in the generation of man, body in common with the animals, and reason and intelligence in common with the gods, many incline to this kinship, which is miserable and mortal; and some few to that which is divine and happy. Since, then, it is of necessity that every man uses everything according to the opinion which he has about it, those, the few, who think that they are formed for fidelity and modesty and a sure use of appearances have no mean or ignoble thoughts about themselves; but with the many it is quite the contrary. For they say, What am I? A poor, miserable man, with my wretched bit of flesh. Wretched, indeed; but you possess something better than your bit of flesh. Why then do you neglect that which is better, and why do you attach yourself to this?

Through this kinship with the flesh, some of us inclining to it become like wolves, faithless and treacherous and mischievous: some become like lions, savage and bestial and untamed; but the greater part of us become foxes, and other worse animals. For what else is a slanderer and a malignant man than a fox, or some other more wretched and meaner animal? See then and take care that you do not become some one of these miserable things.

CIV. If the things are true which are said by the philosophers about the kinship between God and man, what else remains for men to do than what Socrates did? Never, in reply to the question to what country you belong, say that you are an Athenian or a

Corinthian, but that you are a citizen of the world. For why do you say that you are an Athenian, and why do you not say that you belong to the small nook only into which your poor body was cast at birth? Is it not plain that you call yourself an Athenian or Corinthian from the place which has a greater authority and comprises not only that small nook itself and all your family, but even the whole country from which the stock of your progenitors is derived down to you? He, then, who has observed with intelligence the administration of the world, and has learned that the greatest and supreme and the most comprehensive community is that which is composed of men and God, and that from God have descended the seeds not only to my father and grandfather, but to all beings which are generated on the earth and are produced, and particularly to rational beings— for these only are by their nature formed to have communion with God, being by means of reason conjoined with Him — why should not such a man call himself a citizen of the world, why not a son of God, and why should he be afraid of anything which happens among men? Is kinship with Cæsar (the Emperor) or with any other of the powerful in

Rome sufficient to enable us to live in safety, and above contempt and without any fear at all? and to have God for your maker, and father, and guardian, shall not this release us from sorrows and fears?

CV. If we had understanding, ought we to do anything else both jointly and severally than to sing hymns and bless the deity, and to tell of His benefits? Ought we not when we are digging and ploughing and eating to sing this hymn to God? "Great is God, who has given us such implements with which we shall cultivate the earth: great is God, who has given us hands, the power of swallowing, a stomach, imperceptible growth, and the power of breathing while we sleep." This is what we ought to sing on every occasion, and to sing the greatest and most divine hymn for giving us the faculty of comprehending these things and using a proper way. Well then, since most of you have become blind, ought there not to be some man to fill this office, and on behalf of all to sing the hymn to God? For what else can I do, a lame old man, than sing hymns to God? If, then, I were a nightingale, I would do the part of a nightingale. If I were a swan, I would do like a swan.

But now I am a rational creature, and I ought to praise God: this is my work; I do it, nor will I desert this post, so long as I am allowed to keep it; and I exhort you to join in this same song.

CVI. My man, as the proverb says, make a desperate effort on behalf of tranquillity of mind, freedom, and magnanimity. Lift up your head at last as released from slavery. Dare to look up to God and say, Deal with me for the future as Thou wilt; I am of the same mind as Thou art; I am Thine. I refuse nothing that pleases Thee: lead me where Thou wilt: clothe me in any dress Thou choosest. Is it Thy will that I should hold the office of a magistrate, that I should be in the condition of a private man, stay here or be an exile, be poor, be rich? I will make Thy defence to men in behalf of all these conditions: I will shew the nature of each thing what it is. . . . Who would Hercules have been if he had sat at home? He would have been Eurystheus and not Hercules. Well, and in his travels through the world how many intimates and how many friends had he? But nothing more dear to him than God. For this reason it was believed that he was the son of God, and he was. In obedience to God, then, he went about purging away injustice and lawlessness. But you are not Hercules and you are not able to purge away the wickedness of others; nor yet are you Theseus, able to purge away the evil things of Attica. Clear away your own. From yourself, from your thoughts cast away instead of Procrustes and Sciron, sadness, fear, desire, envy, malevolence, avarice, effeminacy, intemperance. But it is not possible to eject these things otherwise than by looking to God only, by fixing your affections on Him only, by being consecrated to His commands. But if you choose anything else, you will with sighs and groans be compelled to follow what is stronger than yourself, always seeking tranquillity and never able to find it; for you seek tranquillity there where it is not, and you neglect to seek it where it is.

CVII. This is the true athlete, the man who exercises himself against such appearances. . . . Great is the combat, divine is the work; it is for kingship, for freedom, for happiness, for freedom from perturbation. Remember God: call on Him as a helper and protector, as men at sea call on the

Dioscuri in a storm. For what is a greater storm than that which comes from appearances which are violent and drive away the reason? For the storm itself, what else is it but an appearance? For take away the fear of death, and suppose as many thunders and lightnings as you please, and you will know what calm and serenity there is in the ruling faculty. But if you have once been defeated and say that you will conquer hereafter, and then say the same again, be assured that you will at last be in so wretched a condition and so weak that you will not even know afterwards that you are doing wrong, but you will even begin to make apologies (defences) for your wrong-doing, and then you will confirm the saying of Hesiod to be true:

"With constant ills the dilatory strives."

CVIII. And how is it possible that a man who has nothing, who is naked, houseless, without a hearth, squalid, without a slave, without a city, can pass a life that flows easily? See, God has sent you a man to show you that it is possible. Look at me, who am without a city, without a house, without possessions, without a slave; I sleep on the ground; I have no wife, no children, no prætorium, but only the earth and heavens, and one poor cloak. And what do I want? Am I not without sorrow? Am I not without fear? Am I not free? When did any of you see me failing in the object of my desire? or ever falling into that which I would avoid? did I ever blame God or man? did I ever accuse any man? did any of you ever see me with sorrowful countenance? And how do I meet with those whom you are afraid of and admire? Do I not treat them like slaves? Who, when he sees me, does not think that he sees his king and master?

CIX. Wherefore the wise and good man, remembering who he is and whence he came, and by whom he was produced, is attentive only to this, how he may fill his place with due regularity, and obediently to God. Dost thou still wish me to exist (live)? I will continue to exist as free, as noble in nature, as thou hast wished me to exist; for thou hast made me free from hindrance in that which is my own. But hast thou no further need of me? I thank thee; and so far I have remained for thy sake, and for the sake of no other person, and now in obedience to thee I depart. How dost thou depart? Again, I say, as thou hast pleased, as free, as thy servant, as one who has known thy commands and thy prohibitions. And so long as I shall stay in thy service, whom dost thou will me to be? A prince or a private man, a senator or a common person, a soldier or a general, a teacher or a master of a family? whatever place and position thou mayest assign to me, as Socrates says, I will die ten thousand times rather than desert them. And where dost thou will me to be? in Rome or Athens, or Thebes or Gyara? Only remember me there where I am. If thou sendest me to a place where there are no means for men living according to nature, I shall not depart (from life) in disobedience to thee, but as if thou wast giving me the signal to retreat: I do not leave thee, let this be far from my intention, but I perceive that thou hast no need of me. If means of living according to nature be allowed to me, I will seek no other place than that in which I am, or other men than those among whom I am.

CX. How do you understand, "attaching yourself to God"? In this sense, that whatever God wills, a man also shall will; and what God does not will, a man also shall not will. How then shall this be done? In what other way than by examining the movements (the acts) of God and His administration? What has He given to me as my own and in my own power? what has He reserved to Himself? He has given to me the things which are in the power of the will: He has put them in my power free from impediment and hindrance. How was He able to make the earthy body free from hindrance? (He could not), and accordingly He has subjected to the revolution of the whole possessions, household things, house, children, wife. Why then do I fight against God? why do I will what does not depend on the will? why do I will to have absolutely what is not granted to me? But how ought I to will to have things? In the way in which they are given and as long as they are given. But He who has given takes away. Why then do I resist? I do not say that I shall be a fool if I use force to one who is stronger, but I shall first be unjust. For whence had I things when I came into the world?—My father gave them to me —And who gave them to him? and who made the sun? and who made the fruits of the earth? and who the seasons? and who made the connection of men with one another and their fellowship?

Then after receiving everything from another and even yourself, are you angry and do you blame the giver if he takes anything from you? Who are you, and for what purpose did you come into the world? Did not He (God) introduce you here, did He not show you the light, did He not give you fellow-workers, and perceptions, and reason? and as whom did He introduce you here? did He not introduce you as subject to death, and as one to live on the earth with a little flesh, and to observe His administration, and to join with Him in the spectacle and the festival for a short time? Will you not then, as long as you have been permitted, after seeing the spectacle and the solemnity, when He leads you out, go with adoration of Him and thanks for what you have heard and seen?—No; but I would still enjoy the feast.—The initiated too would wish to be longer in the initiation: and perhaps also those at Olympia to see other athletes; but the solemnity is ended: go away like a grateful and modest man; make room for others: others also must be born, as you were, and being born they must have a place, and houses and necessary things. And if the first do not retire, what remains? Why are you insatiable? Why are you not content? why do you contract the world?—Yes, but I would have my little children with me and my wife.—What, are they yours? do they not belong to the giver, and to Him who made you? then will you not give up what belongs to others? will you not give way to Him who is superior?

CXI. In the name of the merciful and compassionate God.

Praise belongs to God, the Lord of the worlds, the merciful, the compassionate, the ruler of the day of judgment! Thee we serve and Thee we ask for aid. Guide us in the right path, the path of those Thou art gracious to; not of those Thou art wroth with; nor of those who err.

O ye folk! serve your Lord who created you and those before you; haply ye may fear! who made the earth for you a bed and the heaven a dome; and sent down from heaven water, and brought forth therewith fruits as a sustenance for you; so make no peers for God, the while ye know!

Draw not near to the wealth of the orphan,

save to improve it, until he reaches the age of puberty, and fulfil your compacts; verily a compact is ever inquired of.

And give full measure, when ye measure out, and weigh with a right balance; that is better and a fairer determination.

And do not pursue that of which thou hast no knowledge; verily, the hearing, the sight, and the heart, all of these shall be inquired of.

And walk not on the earth proudly; verily, thou canst not cleave the earth, and thou shalt not reach the mountains in height.

All this is ever evil in the sight of your Lord and abhorred.

O my son! be steadfast in prayer, and bid what is reasonable and forbid what is wrong; be patient of what befalls thee, verily, that is one of the determined affairs.

CXII. O ye who believe! remember God with frequent remembrance, and celebrate His praises morning and evening.

He it is who prays for you and His angels too, to bring you forth out of the darkness into the light, for He is merciful to the believers.

But wait thou patiently for the judgment of thy Lord, for thou art in our eyes. And celebrate the praises of thy Lord what time thou risest, and in the night, and at the fading of the stars!

And on that day no soul shall be wronged at all, nor shall ye be rewarded for aught but that which ye have done.

And every man's augury have we fastened on his neck; and we will bring forth for him on the resurrection day a book offered to him wide open: "Read thy book, thou art accountant enough against thyself to-day!"

In the name of the merciful and compassionate God.
Say, "I seek refuge in the Lord of men, the King of men, the God of men, from the evil of the whisperer, who slinks off, who whispers into the hearts of men."

God, there is no god but He, the living, the self-subsistent. Slumber takes Him not, nor sleep. He is what is in the heavens and what is in the earth. Who is it that intercedes with Him save by His permission? He knows what is before them and what behind them, and they comprehend not aught of His knowledge but of what He pleases. His throne extends over the heavens and the earth, and it tires Him not to guard them both, for He is high and grand.

CXIII. Serve ye none but God, and to your two parents show kindness, and to your kindred and the orphans and the poor, and speak to men kindly, and be steadfast in prayer, and give alms.

O ye who believe! expend in alms of what we have bestowed upon you, before the day comes in which is no barter, and no friendship, and no intercession.

Verily, those who believe, and act righteously, and are steadfast in prayer, and give alms, theirs is their hire with their Lord; there is no fear on them, nor shall they grieve.

Kind speech and pardon are better than almsgiving followed by annoyance, and God is rich and clement.

And never say of anything, "Verily, I am going to do that to-morrow," except "if God please "; and remember thy Lord when thou hast forgotten, and say, "It may be that my Lord will guide me to what is nearer to the right than this."

What shall make thee know what the steep (path) is? It is freeing captives, or feeding, on the day of famine, an orphan who is akin, or a poor man who lies in the dust; and again (it is) to be of those who believe and encourage each other to patience, and encourage each other to mercy—these are the fellows of the right!

God's is what is in the heavens and what is in the earth! and God sufficeth for a guardian!

He who wishes for a reward in this world —with God is the reward of this world and of the next, and God both hears and sees.

O ye who believe! be ye steadfast in justice, witnessing before God though it be against yourselves, or your parents, or your kindred, be it rich or poor, for God is nearer akin than either.

If God were to punish men for their wrongdoing He would not leave upon the earth a single beast; but He respites them until a stated time; and when their time comes they cannot put it off an hour, nor can they bring it on.

CXIV. When the night overshadowed him (Abraham), he saw a star, and said, "This is my Lord"; but when it set he said, "I love not those that set."

And when he saw the moon beginning to rise, he said, "This is my Lord"; but when it set he said, "If God my Lord guides me not, I shall surely be of the people who err."

And when he saw the sun beginning to rise, he said, "This is my Lord; this is greatest of all"; but when it set he said, "O my people! verily I am clear of what ye associate with God; verily, I have turned my face to Him who originated the heaven and the earth."

CXV. Verily, your Lord is God who created the heavens and the earth in six days. He covers night with the day—it pursues it incessantly—and the sun and the moon and the stars are subject to His bidding. Aye! His is the creation and the bidding—blessed be God the Lord of the world!

In the name of the merciful and compassionate God.
Say, "He is God alone!
God the Eternal!
He begets not and is not begotten!
Nor is there like unto Him any one!"

Verily, He produces and returns, and He is the forgiving, the loving, the Lord of the glorious throne; the doer of what He will!

His are what is in the heavens and what is in the earth, and what is between the two, and what is beneath the ground! And if thou art public in thy speech—yet, verily, He knows the secret, and more hidden still.

Verily, thou shalt surely be guided into the right way—the way of God, whose is what is in the heavens and what is in the earth. Ay, to God affairs do tend!

Celebrated be the praises of God, when ye are in the evening and when ye are in the morning! for to Him belongs praise in the heavens and the earth! and at the evening, and when ye are at noon. He brings forth the lining from the cloud, and brings forth the dead from the living: and He quickens the earth after its death, and thus shall ye too be brought forth.

In the name of the merciful and compassionate God.
When the sun is folded up,
And when the stars do fall,
And when the mountains are moved,

. . . . .

And when the seas shall surge up,
And when souls shall be paired with bodies,

. . . . .

And when the pages shall be spread out,
And when the heaven shall be flayed,
And when hell shall be set ablaze,
And when Paradise shall be brought nigh,
The soul shall know what it has produced!

With Him are the keys of the unseen. None knows them save He; He knows what is in the land and in the sea; and there falls not a leaf save that He knows it; nor a grain in the darkness of the earth, nor aught that is moist, nor aught that is dry, save that is in His perspicuous Book.

## c. Religion in Society and the State

## c. Religion in Society and the State

CXVI. The business of government!—ought we not to be earnest in it? ought we not to be earnest in it?

. . . . .

Your Majesty's business is to care reverently for the people.

. . . . .

Heaven loves the people, and the sovereign should reverently carry out (this mind of) Heaven.

. . . . .

He did not dare to indulge in useless ease, but admirably and tranquilly presided over the regions of Yin, till throughout them all, small and great, there was not a single murmur.

. . . . .

When intelligence rules in your cities, then will you be proved to be attentive to your duties.

. . . . .

When his House was in its greatest strength, he sought for able men who should honor God (in the discharge of their duties). (His advisers), when they knew of men thoroughly proved and trustworthy in the practice of the nine virtues, would then presume to inform and instruct their sovereign, saying, "With our hands to our heads and our heads to the ground, O Sovereign, we would say, Let (such an one) occupy one of your high offices."

.        .        .        .        .

You who direct the government and preside over criminal cases through all the land, are you not constituted the shepherds of Heaven?

.        .        .        .        .

Go and reverently exercise the duties of your office.

CXVII. It is given to me, the one man (the Emperor) to secure the harmony and tranquillity of your states and clans; and now I know not whether I may not offend against (the Powers) above and below. I am fearful and trembling, as if I were in danger of falling into a deep abyss. Throughout all the regions that enter on a new life under me, do not (ye princes) follow lawless ways; make no approach to insolence and dissoluteness; let every one be careful to keep his statutes; —that so we may receive the favor of Heaven. The good in you I will not dare to keep concealed; and for the evil in me I will not dare to forgive myself. I will examine these things in harmony with the mind of God. When guilt is found anywhere in you who occupy the myriad regions, let it rest on me, the One man. When guilt is found in me, the One man, it shall not attach to you who occupy the myriad regions.

Oh! let us attain to be sincere in these things, and so we shall likewise have a (happy) consummation.

CXVIII. The sovereign, having established (in himself) the highest degree and pattern of excellence, concentrates in his own person the five (sources of) happiness, and proceeds to diffuse them, and give them to the multitudes of the people. Then they, on their part, embodying your perfection, will give it (back) to you, and secure the preservation of it. Among all the multitudes of the people there will be no unlawful confederacies, and among men (in office) there will be no bad and selfish combinations;—let the sovereign establish in (himself) the highest degree and pattern of excellence.

Among all the multitudes of the people there will be those who have ability to plan and to act, and who keep themselves (from evil): do you keep such in mind; and there will be those who not coming up to the highest point of excellence, yet do not involve themselves in evil:—let the sovereign receive such. And when a placid satisfaction appears on their countenances, and they say, "Our love is fixed on virtue," do you then confer favors on them;—those men will in this way advance to the perfection of the sovereign. Do not let him oppress the friendless and childless, nor let him fear the high and distinguished. When men (in office) have ability and administrative power, let them be made still more to cultivate their conduct; and the prosperity of the country will be promoted. All (such) right men, having a competency, will go on in goodness.

CXIX. The jade uncut will not form a vessel for use; and if men do not learn, they do not know the way (in which they should go). On this account the ancient kings, when establishing states and governing the people, made instruction and schools a primary object;—as it is said in the Charge to Yueh, " The thoughts from first to last should be fixed on learning."

. . . . .

The Master said : The laying the foundation of (all) love in the love of parents teaches people concord. The laying the foundation of (all) reverence in the reverence of elders teaches the people obedience.

. . . . .

With the ancients in their practice of government the love of men was the great point.

. . . . .

Virtue is the root; wealth is the branches. If he make the root his secondary object, and the branches his primary object, he will only quarrel with the people, and teach them rapine.

The ancients who wished to illustrate illustrious virtue throughout the kingdom first ordered well their states. Wishing to order well their states, they first regulated their families. Wishing to regulate their families, they first cultivated their persons. Wishing to cultivate their persons, they first rectified their hearts. Wishing to rectify their hearts, they first sought to be sincere in their thoughts. Wishing to be sincere in their thoughts, they first extended to the utmost their knowledge.

CXX. And the community which has neither poverty nor riches will always have the noblest principles; there is no insolence or injustice, nor, again, are there any contentions or envyings among them.

For no man ought to have pre-eminent honor in a state because he surpasses others in wealth, any more than because he is swift, or fair, or strong, unless he have some virtue in him; nor even if he have virtue, unless he have this particular virtue of temperance.

We must hearken, both in private and public life, and regulate our cities and houses according to law, meaning by the very term "law," the distribution of mind.

Now, according to our view, such governments are not polities at all, nor are laws right which are passed for the good of particular classes and not for the good of the whole state.

For that state in which the law is subject and has no authority, I perceive to be on the highway to ruin; but I see that the state in which the law is above the rulers, and the rulers are the inferiors of the law, has salvation, and every blessing which the gods can confer.

Worthy of honor, too, is he who does no injustice, and of more than two-fold honor if he not only does no injustice himself, but hinders others from doing any; the first may count as one man, the second is worth many men, because he informs the rulers of the injustice of others. And yet more highly to be esteemed is he who co-operates with the rulers in correcting the citizens as far as he can—he shall be proclaimed the great and perfect citizen, and bear away the palm of virtue.

"Friends," we say to them,—"God, as the old tradition declares, holding in His hand the beginning, middle, and end of all that is, moves according to His nature in a straight line towards the accomplishment of His end. Justice always follows Him, and is the punisher of those who fall short of the divine law. To that law, he who would be happy holds fast, and follows it in all humility and order; but he who is lifted up with pride, or money, or honor, or beauty, who has a soul hot with folly, and youth, and insolence, and thinks that he has no need of a guide or ruler, but is able himself to be the guide of others, he, I say, is left deserted of God; and being thus deserted, he takes to him others who are like himself, and dances about, throwing all things into confusion, and many think that he is a great man, but in a short time he pays a penalty which justice cannot but approve, and is utterly destroyed, and his family and city with him. Wherefore, seeing that human things are thus ordered, what should a wise man do or think, or not do or think "?

CXXI. From him I received the idea of a polity in which there is the same law for all, a polity administered with regard to equal rights and equal freedom of speech, and the idea of a kingly government which respects most of all the freedom of the governed.

Every moment think steadily as a Roman and a man to do what thou hast in hand with perfect and simple dignity, and feeling of affection, and freedom and justice; and to give thyself relief from all other thoughts.

My city and country, so far as I am Antoninus, is Rome, but so far as I am a man, it is the world. The things, then, which are useful to these cities are alone useful to me.

For we are made for co-operation, like feet, like hands, like eyelids, like the rows of the upper and lower teeth. To act against one another, then, is contrary to nature.

The intelligence of the universe is social. Accordingly it has made the inferior things for the sake of the superior, and it has fitted the superior to one another. Thou seest how it has subordinated, co-ordinated, and assigned to everything its proper portion, and has brought together into concord with one another the things which are the best.

All things are implicated with one another, and the bond is holy; and there is hardly anything unconnected with any other thing. For things have been co-ordinated, and they combine to form the same universe (order). For there is one universe made up of all things, and one god who pervades all things, and one substance, and one law, (one) common reason in all intelligent animals, and one truth; if indeed there is also one perfection for all animals which are of the same stock and participate in the same reason.

Men exist for the sake of one another. Teach them, then, or bear with them.

As thou thyself art a component part of a social system, so let every act of thine be a component part of social life. Whatever act of thine, then, has no reference either immediately or remotely to a social end, this tears asunder thy life, and does not allow it to be one, and it is of the nature of a mutiny just as when in a popular assembly a man acting by himself stands apart from the general agreement.

CXXII. Wealth is not one of the good things; great expenditure is one of the bad; moderation is one of the good things. And moderation invites to frugality and the acquisition of good things: but wealth invites to great expenditure and draws us away from moderation. It is difficult, then, for a rich man to be moderate, or for a moderate man to be rich.

As he who is in health would not choose to be served (ministered to) by the sick, nor for those who dwell with him to be sick, so neither would a free man endure to be served by slaves, or for those who live with him to be slaves.

If you wish your house to be well managed, imitate the Spartan Lycurgus. For as he did not fence his city with walls, but fortified the inhabitants by virtue and preserved the city always free; so do you not cast around (your house) a large court and raise high towers, but strengthen the dwellers by good will and fidelity and friendship, and then nothing harmful will enter it, not even if the whole band of wickedness shall array itself against it.

If you propose to adorn your city by the dedication of offerings (monuments), first dedicate to yourself (decorate yourself with) the noblest offering of gentleness, and justice, and beneficence.

You will do the greatest services to the

state, if you shall raise not the roofs of the houses, but the souls of the citizens: for it is better that great souls should dwell in small houses than for mean slaves to lurk in great houses.

Do not decorate the walls of your house with the valuable stones from Eubœa and Sparta; but adorn the minds (breasts) of the citizens and of those who administer the state with the instruction which comes from Hellas (Greece). For states are well governed by the wisdom (judgment) of men, but not by stone and wood.

As, if you wished to breed lions, you would not care about the costliness of their dens, but about the habits of the animals; so, if you attempt to preside over your citizens, be not so anxious about the costliness of the buildings as careful about the manly character of those who dwell in them.

Every place is safe to him who lives with justice.

Law intends indeed to do service to human life, but it is not able when men do not choose to accept her services; for it is only in those who are obedient to her that she displays her special virtue.

As to the sick, physicians are as saviours, so to those also who are wronged are the laws.

The justest laws are those which are the truest.

CXXIII. I am a man, and nothing that concerns human beings is indifferent to me.

We are by nature inclined to love mankind. Take away love and benevolence, and you take away all the joy of life. Men are born for the sake of men, that they may mutually benefit one another.

When man shall have studied the nature of all things, and shall come to look upon himself as not confined within the walls of one city, or as a member of any particular community, but as a citizen of the universe considered as one Commonwealth—amid such an acquaintance with Nature, and such a grand magnificence of things, to what a knowledge of himself will man attain!

Give bread to a stranger in the name of

the universal brotherhood which binds all men together, under the common Father of Nature.

Nature fitted us for social life by planting within us a mutual love. We are members of one great body; and we must consider that we were born for the good of the whole.

I will look upon the whole world as my country, and upon God as both the witness and judge of my actions. I will live and die with this testimony— that I never invaded another man's freedom, and that I preserved my own.

The universe is but one great city full of beloved ones, divine and human by nature endeared to each other.

The law imprinted on the hearts of all men is to love the members of society as themselves. The eternal, universal, unchangeable law of all beings is to seek the good of one another, like children of the same Father.

# II

# Prayers

## A. Collects of Universality

# II

# Prayers

## A. Collects of Universality

I. Our God, and God of our fathers! May Thy presence be manifest to us in all Thy works, and may reverence for Thee fill the hearts of all Thy creatures; may all the children of men bow before Thee in humility and unite to do Thy will with perfect hearts, and all acknowledge that Thine is the kingdom, the power, and the majesty, and that Thy name is exalted above all.

Grant hope, O LORD, to them that seek Thee; inspire with courage all who wait for Thee, and be nigh unto all who trust in Thy name; that all men may walk in the light of Thy truth, and recognize that they are children of One Father, that One God has created them all. Then shall the just rejoice and the righteous be glad; then shall iniquity be no more and all men will render homage to Thee alone as their God and King.

Eternal, our God, may Thy kingdom come speedily, and the worship of Thy name and obedience to Thy law unite all men in the bonds of brotherhood and peace, that every creature may know that Thou hast created it, and every living being exclaim: The Eternal, the God of Israel, ruleth, and His dominion endureth forever. *Amen.*

II. We most earnestly beseech Thee, O Thou lover of mankind, to be mindful of the one holy Catholic Church, which is spread over the face of the whole earth: be mindful, O LORD, of all Thy people, the flocks of Thy fold. . . .

O King of Peace, give us Thy peace; keep us in love and charity; be our God, for we know none besides Thee; we call upon Thy name; grant unto our souls the life of righteousness, that the death of sin may not prevail against us, or any of Thy people. . . .

Relieve those who are in prisons or in the mines, under accusations or condemnations, in exile or in slavery, or loaded with grievous tribute; deliver them all, for Thou art our

God, who loosest those who are in bonds, and raisest up those who are oppressed; the hope of the hopeless, the helper of the helpless, the lifter up of those who are fallen, the haven of those who are shipwrecked, the avenger of those who are injured. . . . And, O Lord, Thou physician of soul and body, heal all our infirmities both of soul and body: O Thou, who art the overseer of all flesh, watch over us and heal us by Thy saving health. . . .

Bless also, O Lord, and crown the year with the riches of Thy goodness, for the sake of the poor, the widow, the fatherless, and the stranger; for the sake of all of us, who put our trust in Thee, and call upon Thy holy name: for the eyes of all wait upon Thee, O Lord, and Thou givest them their meat in due season. . . .

Give rest to the souls of our fathers and brethren, O Lord our God, in the tabernacles of Thy saints; dispense unto them in Thy Kingdom those good things which Thou hast promised, which eye hath not seen, nor ear heard, neither have entered into the heart of man, which Thou hast prepared, O God, for those who love Thy holy name. Give rest to their souls, and vouchsafe them the kingdom of heaven: but grant unto us that we may finish our lives as well pleasing to Thee, and free from sin, and that we may have our portion and lot with all Thy saints. *Amen.*

III. We are met, O LORD, in Thy name, to inquire the law from Thy mouth, and seek those things which make for the peace of Jerusalem; and since all our profiting depends upon Thy blessing, fulfil to us, we beseech Thee, Thy gracious promise that where two or three of Thy disciples are gathered together in Thy name, Thou wilt be in the midst of them. Vouchsafe to preside over this assembly by Thy Spirit, the Spirit of truth and peace. Sanctify us in Thy truth. Purify and enlighten our minds, that we may truly understand, and devoutly handle, Thy Holy Word. Suffer us not, O LORD, to deceive any man by the Scriptures, nor let us be ourselves deceived; but grant that, seeking the truth sincerely, we may find it, and having found it, may hold it fast with a steady faith. Oh, that we may all praise Thee, with one mouth and one mind, and that there may be no divisions among us; and help us at the same time to remember that the contention which unites us to God is better than the peace which separates us from Him. Bring back into the right way any that have erred and been deceived. May the peace of God which passeth understanding keep our hearts and minds in the knowledge and love of the truth; and may the blessing of God Almighty, . . . be upon and abide with us henceforth and evermore, world without end. *Amen.*

IV. O God, who art, and wast, and art to come, before whose face the generations rise and pass away; age after age the living seek Thee, and find that of Thy faithfulness there is no end. Our fathers in their pilgrimage walked by Thy guidance, and rested on Thy compassion: still to their children be Thou the cloud by day, the fire by night. Where but in Thee have we a covert from storm or shadow from the heat of life ? In our manifold temptations, Thou alone knowest and art ever nigh: in sorrow, Thy pity revives the fainting soul: in our prosperity and ease, it is Thy Spirit only that can wean us from our pride and keep us low.

O Thou sole source of peace and righteousness; take now the veil from every heart: and join us in one communion with Thy prophets and saints who have trusted in Thee, and were not ashamed. Not of our worthiness, but of Thy tender mercy, hear our prayer. *Amen.*

V. O God, who art the unsearchable abyss of peace, the ineffable sea of love, the fountain of blessings, and the bestower of affection, who sendest peace to those that receive it, open to us this day the sea of Thy love, and water us with plenteous streams from the riches of Thy grace, and from the most sweet springs of Thy benignity. Make us children of quietness and heirs of peace. Enkindle in us the fire of Thy love; sow in us Thy fear; strengthen our weakness by Thy power; bind us closely to Thee and to each other in one firm and indissoluble bond of unity. *Amen.*

VI. O Thou that makest both light and darkness, Thine is also the light invisible, the revelation of God to our souls.

All writings of law, and oracles of prophets, all music of Psalms, and instruction of Proverbs, Hebrew and Gentile, these all are rays from Thy fountain, Sun invisible and spiritual, with whom is no night forever.

God is the Eternal, who shows us light: bind the sacrifice of our hearts with the cords of good will.

Let us rise, as the Truth of God rises, to newness of life, who can bring again from the dead those who are buried in sorrow and slain by sin; and can perfect us in every good work, to do His will, to whom be glory forever. *Amen.*

VII. Almighty and everlasting God, the Brightness of faithful souls, . . . fill the world with Thy glory, and shew Thyself by the radiance of Thy light to the nations that are subject unto Thee. . . . *Amen.*

VIII. Arise, O LORD, who judgest the earth; and as Thou dwellest in and possessest the faith of all nations, suffer us not to abide in darkness; and grant that we may not lay the foundations of our faith on the sand where the whirlwind may overthrow them, but be established on the rock which is steadfast in Thee. *Amen.*

IX. Blessed be Thou, O LORD, who bringest forth on earth, and out of earth, wild creatures, bird, and beast, and creeping thing, and makest man after Thy likeness, to rule the earth, and crownest him with blessing.

Thine is our breath, and Thine our likeness; counsel to desire, and hand to fashion, come of Thee. . . .

From Thee came ancient revelation and writing; deep sayings of prophets, and songs of praise.

From Thee are all the wise sayings of old time; the experience of story, and worship of prayer and offering.

In the blind struggles of men is the promise of Thy truth; and in fulness of time fulfilment, when out of evil comes good, and patience ends in victory. . . .

By the agony of mankind striving; by men's heads bowed in shame, and eyes filled with tears; by their necks weighed down with burdens, their feet and hands perplexed and bound; by their hearts often pierced, and tears of blood flowing; and by their strong crying out of misery to their God: be moved, O Lord, to arise and amend the earth. . . .

Save us from enmity and strife, from all malice and envying, from religious blindness and faction, and from brooding of evil temper.

Give us, O Lord, things holy, calm, and blessed; love, joy, and peace. . . .

Pour out the gifts of the ever-living God, words of wisdom, knowledge, and charity, gifts of healing and working wonders on men's hearts, the clear eye of truth and discerning of spirits, a learned tongue, and interpretation of tongues. . . .

By the indwelling of Thy breath of holiness, peace, and truth, hallow us, and in the fellowship of godly men strengthen us.

By pure religious rites consecrate us, and let their inner meaning cleanse us, that our scars of soul may be healed, and the wounds of sin done away.

And let the peace of God, which passeth understanding, keep our hearts and thoughts in the knowledge and love of God. *Amen.*

X. O God, who hast taught Thy Church to keep all Thy heavenly commandments by loving Thy Godhead and our neighbor; grant us the spirit of peace and grace, that Thy universal family may be both devoted to Thee with their whole heart, and united to each other with a pure will. . . . *Amen.*

XI. O God, who art Peace everlasting,

whose chosen reward is the gift of peace, and who hast taught us that the peacemakers are Thy children, pour Thy sweet peace into our souls, that everything discordant may utterly vanish, and all that makes for peace be sweet to us forever. *Amen.*

XII. O everlasting Teacher of mankind, from Thee come the workers of good forever.

Thine are the revivers of godliness in the world, and the sowers of winged seeds of truth.

Thine, O LORD, is the great company of our ancestors, the sacred truth-tellers, and glorious patriots.

All makers of story and song, and the masters of harmony are Thine, and the pure sufferers for godliness.

Whoever have vanquished evil, and in faith and hope gone through labor for right:

Dost not Thou count their blood precious, O LORD, and remember all their tears?

Glory to Thee, LORD, for Thy Spirit in them; and in their spirit let us praise Thee. *Amen.*

XIII. Dissolve, O LORD, the schisms of

heresy, which seek to subvert the faith, which strive to corrupt the truth; that as Thou art acknowledged in heaven and in earth as one and the same Lord, so Thy people, gathered from all nations, may serve Thee in the unity of faith. *Amen.*

XIV. We give thanks to Thee, O LORD God, Father Almighty; . . . and we offer unto Thee this reasonable . . . service, which all nations offer unto Thee, O LORD, from the rising of the sun unto the going down thereof, from the north and from the south;—for great is Thy Name in all nations, and in every place incense and sacrifice and oblation are offered unto Thy holy Name. *Amen.*

XV. O God, of unchangeable power and eternal light, look favorably on Thy whole Church, that wonderful and sacred mystery; and, by the tranquil operation of Thy perpetual Providence, carry out the work of man's salvation; and let the whole world feel and see that things which were cast down are being raised up, and things which had grown old are being made new, and all things are returning to perfection through Him from whom they took their origin. . . . *Amen.*

XVI. O Eternal Spirit, who hast made the nearness of God to man the beginning of all religion, grant us in all love and obedience to be reckoned Thy children, through that holy breathing of God, whereby the whole family of mankind is joined into one and sanctified. *Amen.*

XVII. O God, the Enlightener of all nations, pour into our hearts that light which scatters all perplexity of sin, and grant Thy people to enjoy perpetual peace. *Amen.*

XVIII. O LORD, who hast taught us that all our doings without charity are nothing worth; send Thy Holy Ghost, and pour into our hearts that most excellent gift of charity, the very bond of peace and of all virtues, without which whosoever liveth is counted dead before Thee. . . . *Amen.*

XIX. Grant unto us, O LORD God, that we may love one another unfeignedly; for where love is, there art Thou; and he that loveth his brother is born of Thee, and dwelleth in Thee, and Thou in him. And where brethren do glorify Thee with one accord, there dost Thou pour out Thy blessing upon them. Love us, therefore, O LORD, and shed Thy love into our hearts, that we may love Thee, and our brethren in Thee and for Thee, as all children to Thee. . . . *Amen.*

XX. Blessed LORD, who hast caused all true records and holy songs to be written for our learning; we thank Thee for signs of Thy providence and inspiration . . . in many lands; and we desire of Thee the gifts of patience, soberness, and wisdom, so to read the letter of things written in old time, that Thy Holy Spirit of truth may ever live in us; and that we may so remember the story of things temporal, as ever to worship the unseen God, who is eternal. *Amen.*

XXI. Ah, LORD God, Thou Holy Lover of our souls, when Thou comest into our souls, all that is within us shall rejoice. Thou art our Glory and the exultation of our hearts; Thou art our Hope and Refuge in the day of our trouble. Set us free from all evil passions, and heal our hearts of all inordinate affections; that, being inwardly cured and thoroughly cleansed, we may be made fit to love, courageous to suffer, steady to persevere. Nothing is sweeter than Love, nothing more courageous, nothing fuller nor better in heaven and earth; because Love is born of God, and cannot rest but in God, above all created things. Let us love Thee more than ourselves, nor love ourselves but for Thee; and in Thee all that truly love Thee, as the law of Love commandeth, shining out from Thyself. . . . *Amen.*

XXII. O Thou who art love and dwellest in love! teach us herein to be followers of Thee, as dear children. Never may we shut our hearts against the sorrows of even the unthankful and the evil. Make us organs of Thy tender mercy, to soothe the wretched, to lift the penitent, to seek and to save the lost; till all shall at length know themselves Thy children, and be one with each other and with Thee. *Amen.*

XXIII. O LORD God, Father Almighty, we . . . offer unto Thee this service of our spirits and oblation of our minds, which Thy chosen servants in all nations, from sunrise to sunset, and from pole to pole, ever offer to Thee, the Father of our spirits; for there is neither nation nor tongue where Thy Spirit is not known; and in every place the incense of sighs, and the sacrifice of love, and the offering of man's soul, is dear in Thy sight. *Amen.*

XXIV. O God, who hast taught us to keep all Thy heavenly commandments by loving Thee and our neighbor; grant us the spirit of peace and grace that we may be both devoted to Thee with our whole heart, and united to each other with a pure will. . . . *Amen.*

XXV. O Blessed LORD, who hast commanded us to love one another, grant us grace that, having received Thine undeserved bounty, we may love every one in Thee and for Thee. We implore Thy clemency for all; but especially for the friends whom Thy love has given to us. Love Thou them, O Thou Fountain of love, and make them to love Thee with all their heart, that they may will, and speak, and do those things only which are pleasing to Thee. *Amen.*

XXVI. O Living God our Father, who in mankind makest Thyself known by Thy Word, binding men by Thy breath into one, giving us sonship as sons, though we owe to

Thee as Lord the faithfulness of servants: mayest Thou breathe on us holier power, and unite us to Thyself and to our brethren, of every name, color, and opinion, with sympathy in all sanctity and right, with faith of sins forgiven, a lively hope of rising out of every evil, and of eternal life before God. *Amen.*

XXVII. O God our Father, Good beyond all that is good, Fair beyond all that is fair, in whom is calmness and peace; do Thou make up the dissensions which divide us from each other, and bring us back into an unity of love, which may bear some likeness to Thy sublime nature. Grant that we may be spiritually one, as well in ourselves as in each other, through that peace of Thine which maketh all things peaceful. . . . *Amen.*

XXVIII. From strife in our prayers, and perplexity in our teachings, and from all false and deadening interpretations;

From superstitious and ungodly teaching, and from innovation in things unchangeable;

From all pride of ignorance, or of knowledge, and from the tyranny of the unlearned or the worldly;

From darkening counsel with words, and

from remembering our differences with men, till we forget our God;

From all anarchy and tyranny, and from confusion of mind, family, and state, enlighten and deliver us, LORD.

From the loss of wise counsellors in Church and State, and from growing weary of Thy holy word and will;

From all bereavement, sorrow, and desertion; from all things that separate us from each other and from our God;

From all evils we have prayed against, and from all we have not thought of, deliver, O LORD, Thy servants, whose hope is in Thy goodness forever. *Amen.*


XXIX. LORD, make us to resemble even here the heavenly kingdom, through mutual love, where all hatred is quite banished, and all is full of love, and, consequently, full of joy and gladness. *Amen.*


XXX. O God, since Thou art Love, and he that loveth not Thee and his brethren knoweth Thee not and abideth in death, deliver us from injustice, envy, hatred, and malice; give us grace to pardon all who have offended us, and to bear with one another, even as Thou, LORD, dost bear with us, in Thy patience and great loving-kindness. *Amen.*

XXXI. To Thee all nations cry aloud, who hast many names and one nature; the one helper of all, and all things to all men.

Thou who knowest each man and his prayer, every house and its need; . . .

Put away the religious quarrels of ignorance and pride: break the oppressor's rod, and silence them that rule by lies.

Teach men in peace to understand each other's dissonant cries, and receive all nations into Thy kingdom.

Let us dwell with Thee in peace, as children of light: and in Thy light, LORD, let us see light. *Amen.*

XXXII. O God, who through the grace of Thy Holy Spirit dost pour the gift of love into the hearts of Thy faithful people, grant unto us health, both of mind and body, that we love Thee with our whole strength, and with entire satisfaction may perform those things which are pleasing unto Thee. . . . *Amen.*

XXXIII. We most earnestly beseech Thee,

O Thou lover of mankind, to bless all Thy people, the flocks of Thy fold. Send down into our hearts the peace of heaven, and grant us also the peace of this life. Give life to the souls of all of us, and let no deadly sin prevail against us, or any of Thy people. Deliver all who are in trouble, for Thou art our God, who settest the captives free; who givest hope to the hopeless, and help to the helpless; who liftest up the fallen; and who art the Haven of the shipwrecked. Give Thy pity, pardon, and refreshment to every . . . soul, whether in affliction or error. Preserve us, in our pilgrimage through this life, from hurt and danger, and grant that we may end our lives as . . . well pleasing to Thee and free from sin, and that we may have our portion and lot with all Thy saints. *Amen.*

XXXIV. Confirm, O LORD, in our minds the true faith, that as we confess the Divine Thought to be brought forth in mankind by the Breath of God quickening us, so by growing in the same Divine likeness we may be enabled to attain to eternal joy. *Amen.*

XXXV. O God, Who art Peace everlasting,

whose chosen reward is the gift of peace, and who hast taught us that the peace-makers are Thy children, pour Thy peace into our souls, that everything discordant may utterly vanish, and all that makes for peace be sweet to us forever. *Amen.*

XXXVI. O God, Fountain of love, pour Thy love into our souls, that we may love those whom Thou lovest, with the love Thou givest us, and think and speak of them tenderly, meekly, lovingly; and so loving our brethren and sisters for Thy sake, may grow in Thy love, and dwelling in love may dwell in Thee. . . . *Amen.*

XXXVII. We love Thee, O our God; and we desire to love Thee more and more. Grant to us that we may love Thee as much as we desire, and as much as we ought. O dearest Friend, who hast so loved and saved us, the thought of whom is so sweet and always growing sweeter, come and dwell in our hearts; then Thou wilt keep a watch over our lips, our steps, our deeds, and we shall not need to be anxious either for our souls or our bodies. Give us love, sweetest of all gifts, which knows no enemy. Give us in our hearts pure love, born of Thy love to us, that we may love others as Thou lovest us. O most loving Father . . . from whom floweth all love, let our hearts, frozen in sin, cold to Thee and cold to others, be warmed by this divine fire. . . . *Amen.*

XXXVIII. O God, who art the great deep of eternal peace, and the vast sea of love, and the fountain of all blessings, and ever sendest peace upon men of peace, open to us this day the sea of Thy love, and water us with plenteous streams from the riches of Thy grace and from the fresh springs of Thy benignity. Make us children of quietness and heirs of peace. Enkindle in us the fire of Thy love; sow in us Thy fear; strengthen our weakness by Thy power; bind us closely to Thee and to each other in a holy bond of unity. *Amen.*

XXXIX. O Almighty God, help us to put away all bitterness and wrath and evil-speaking, with all malice. May we possess our souls in patience, however we are tempted and provoked, and not be overcome with evil, but overcome evil with good. Enable us, O God of patience, to bear one another's burdens, and to forbear one another in love.

Oh, teach and help us all to live in peace and to love in truth, following peace with all men and walking in love. . . . Subdue all bitter resentments in our minds, and let the law of kindness be in our tongues, and a meek and quiet spirit in all our lives. Make us so gentle and peaceable that we may be followers of Thee as dear children, that Thou, the God of peace, mayest dwell with us forevermore. *Amen.*

XI. LORD our God, who has bidden the light to shine out of darkness, who hast again wakened us to praise Thy goodness and ask for Thy grace: accept now, in Thy endless mercy, the sacrifice of our worship and thanksgiving, and grant unto us all such requests as may be wholesome for us. Make us to be children of the light and of the day, and heirs of Thy everlasting inheritance. Remember, O LORD, according to the multitude of Thy mercies, Thy whole Church; all who join with us in prayer; all our brethren by land or sea, or wherever they may be in Thy vast kingdom, who stand in need of Thy grace and succor. Pour out upon them the riches of Thy mercy, so that we, redeemed in soul and body, and steadfast in faith, may ever praise Thy wonderful and holy name. *Amen.*

XLI. O God of love, and giver of concord, who hast given us counsel for our profit, with a blessed commandment to love one another, even as Thou lovest us, the unworthy and the wandering, and givest us the power of returning to life and salvation; we pray Thee, LORD, give us Thy servants, in all time of our life on the earth (but especially now), a mind forgetful of past ill will, a pure conscience, and sincere thoughts, and a heart to love our brethren. *Amen.*

XLII. O God, our heavenly Father, who hast commanded us to love one another as Thy children, and hast ordained the highest friendship in the bond of Thy Spirit, we beseech Thee to maintain and preserve us always in the same bond, to Thy glory, and our mutual comfort, with all those to whom we are bound by any special tie, either of nature or of choice; that we may be perfected together in that love which is from above, and which never faileth when all other things shall fail. Send down the dew of Thy heavenly grace upon us, that we may have joy in each other that passeth not away; and having lived together in love here, according to Thy commandment, may live forever together with them, being made one in Thee, in Thy glorious kingdom hereafter. *Amen.*

XLIII. O Sovereign and Almighty Lord, bless all Thy people and all Thy flock. Give Thy peace, Thy help, Thy love unto us Thy servants, the sheep of Thy fold, that we may be united in the bond of peace and love, one body and one spirit, in one hope of our calling, in Thy divine and boundless love. *Amen.*

XLIV. O Fount of wisdom! Light of lights! Who knowest every instant more than we could learn in everlasting years! may every opening of truth be to us as a glimpse of Thee. Yet let not our deep ignorance be as the hiding of Thy face, but only as a call to trust Thee, that Thou wilt lead the blind by a way that they knew not. Whatever else thou mayest withhold from us, O give us purity of heart to see Thee, and to trace Thy word within our spirits, and follow Thy footsteps though they lose us in the mighty deep. . . . Bind us to one another, O Thou

Holiest, by a common search for Thy ways and thirsting for Thy Spirit; and raise us to some worthiness of the communion we seek with Thy prophets and saints of every age. Day by day liken us more to the spirits of the departed wise and good; and fit us in our generation to carry on their work below till we are ready for more perfect union with them above. *Amen.*

XLV. O God the Father, and first Author of all divine being, Good beyond all that is good, and Fair beyond all that is fair; in whom is calmness, peace, and concord; do Thou make up the dissensions which divide us from each other, and bring us back into an unity of love, which may bear some likeness to Thy blessed Nature. And as Thou art above all things, make us one by the fellowship of a good mind, that through bonds of affection we may be spiritually one, as well in ourselves as in each other, through that peace of Thine which maketh all things peaceful, and through the grace, mercy, and tenderness wherewith Thou, O Lord, art our Father forever. *Amen.*

XLVI. O Lord, grant to us so to love Thee

with all our heart, with all our mind, and all our soul, and our neighbor for Thy sake; that the grace of charity and brotherly love may dwell in us, and all envy, harshness, and ill will may die in us; and fill our hearts with feelings of love, kindness, and compassion, so that, by constantly rejoicing in the happiness and good success of others, by sympathizing with them in their sorrows, and putting away all harsh judgments and envious thoughts, we may follow Thee, Who art Thyself the true and perfect Love. *Amen.*

XLVII. By that forgiving tenderness, O LORD, wherewith Thou didst ever wait for us; by that tender love wherewith, whenever we wandered, Thou watchest over us; by Thine infinite love, wherewith Thou willest that we should love Thee eternally; give us love like Thine, that we may forgive, compassionate, love like Thee. *Amen.*

XLVIII. O God of unchangeable power and eternal light, look favorably on the whole body of those in whom Thy Holy Spirit dwells, and by Thy perpetual providence carry out the work of man's salvation; that all manner of tyranny and wrong may be cast down, and things which had grown old be made new, and all things return to perfection, through Him from whom they took their origin; even through the Word of Thy Counsel, and the Breathing of Thy Life, who art the living God. *Amen.*

XLIX. Our heavenly Father, we rejoice in the blessed communion of all Thy saints, wherein Thou givest us also to have part. We remember before Thee all who have departed this life in Thy faith and love, and especially those most dear to us. We thank Thee for our present fellowship with them, for our common hope, and for the promise of future joy. Oh, let the cloud of witnesses, the innumerable company of those who have gone before, and entered into rest, be to us for an example of godly life, and even now may we be refreshed with their joy; that so with patience we may run the race that yet remains before us, . . . and obtain an entrance into the everlasting kingdom, the glorious assembly of the saints, and with them ever worship and adore Thy glorious Name, world without end. *Amen.*

L. O God, perfect us in love, that we

may conquer all selfishness and hatred of others; fill our hearts with Thy joy, and shed abroad in them Thy peace which passeth understanding; that so those murmurings and disputings to which we are too prone may be overcome. Make us long-suffering and gentle, and thus subdue our hastiness and angry tempers, and grant that we may bring forth the blessed fruits of the Spirit, to Thy praise and glory. . . . *Amen.*

LI. Pour upon us, O LORD, the spirit of brotherly kindness and peace; so that, sprinkled with the dew of Thy benediction, we may be made glad by Thy glory and grace. . . *Amen.*

LII. Blessed God, who hast caused all good books for our learning, as Thou givest all good thoughts for our thinking, grant us not to misuse any gift of Thy wisdom or of Thy breath. So let us read all holy books carefully, and listen to wise teaching modestly, and meditate on good sayings profitably, and let no pride or bodily humor harden our hearts; but above all, by the true presence of Thy holy Breath, and by Thy constant blessing on all our words and works, lead us into Thy Truth, and give us Thy Peace, which the world cannot give. *Amen.*

LIII. O LORD, make us to love Thee and each other in Thee, and to meet before Thee to dwell in Thine everlasting love. *Amen.*

LIV. O God of love, who hast given a new commandment, . . . that we should love one another, even as Thou didst love us, the unworthy and the wandering, . . . we pray Thee, LORD, give to us Thy servants, in all time of our life on the earth, a mind forgetful of past ill will, a pure conscience, and sincere thoughts, and a heart to love our brethren. *Amen.*

LV. Almighty LORD our God, direct our steps into the way of peace, and strengthen our hearts to obey Thy commands; may the dayspring visit us from on high, and give light to those who sit in darkness and the shadow of death; that they may adore Thee for Thy mercy, follow Thee for Thy truth, and enjoy Thee in Thy sweetness forever. *Amen.*

LVI. O God, our Father, . . . give

us grace seriously to lay to heart the great dangers we are in by our unhappy divisions. Take away from us all hatred and prejudice, and whatsoever else may hinder us from godly union and concord; that as there is but one body, and one Spirit, and one hope of our calling, one Lord, one faith, one baptism, one God and Father of us all, so we may henceforth be all of one heart, and of one soul, united in one holy bond of truth and peace, of faith and charity, and may with one mind and one mouth glorify Thee. . . . *Amen.*

LVII. Break, O LORD, the bonds of all tyranny which enslave the faith, and scatter all superstitions which corrupt the truth; that as Thou art acknowledged in heaven and in earth as one Lord, so Thy people, gathered from all nations, may serve Thee in unity of faith. *Amen.*

LVIII. O Eternal God, who gavest to the Greek a lyre, and to the Romans a sword, suffering the wise of Hellas to behold beauty, and the strong men of Rome to govern the world; yet Thou, when both had fallen from Thee by evil lusts and selfishness, didst cast off both alike, and give them over to delusion and slavery: Grant us grace in Thy holy fear to learn, that by the Spirit of our God is understanding; and, whereas, through our own perverseness we are entangled and hindered in running the race of all virtue which is set before us, raise up, we pray Thee, Thy power, and come among us, and with great might succor us, that, being delivered from an evil mind and enlightened by Thy Holy Spirit, we may both know our duty, and perform the same to Thy honor, who art our living strength and our Lord. *Amen.*

LIX. Almighty God, direct our steps into the way of peace, and strengthen our hearts to obey Thy commands. May the dayspring from on high visit us, and give light to those who sit in darkness and the shadow of death, that they may adore Thee for Thy mercy, follow Thee for Thy truth, and enjoy Thee in Thy sweetness forever. Deliver all nations, we pray Thee, from tyranny and superstition, and from mingling the truth with lies, and . . . gather them into the free assembly of the godly, to the glory and praise of Thy name. *Amen.*

LX. O God of unchangeable power and

eternal light, look favorably on Thy whole Church, and by the quiet operation of Thy perpetual providence, carry out, we beseech Thee, the work of man's salvation; let the whole world feel and see that Thou dost raise up the things which were cast down, and dost make new the things which had grown old, and dost bring all things to their perfection through Him from whom at first they came. . . . *Amen.*

LXI. Our Father who art in heaven, and on earth, we thank Thee that while Thou drawest near unto us, we may draw near unto Thee, and in Thee live and move and have our being. May the words of our mouths and the meditations of our hearts be acceptable in Thy sight, O Lord, our Strength and our Redeemer.

We thank Thee that Thou hast nowhere left Thyself without a witness, but everywhere makest revelations of Thyself, where day unto day uttereth speech of Thee, and night unto night showeth knowledge; yea, where there is no other voice nor language, Thou, Lord, speakest, in Thine infinite wisdom and Thy boundless love. . . .

We thank Thee for the noble institutions

which have come down to us; for the Church, with its many words of truth and its recollections of ancient piety; for the state, with its wise laws; for the community, which puts its hospitable walls around us from the day of our birth, until we are cradled again in our coffin, and the sides of the pit are sweet to our crumbling flesh.

We remember before Thee the ages that are past and gone, and thank Thee for the great men whom Thou causedst to spring up in those days, great flowers of humanity, whose seeds have been scattered broadcast along the world, making the solitary place into a garden, and the wilderness to blossom like a rose. . . .

Yea, we thank Thee for the goodly fellowship of all these prophets of glory, the glorious company of such apostles, and the noble army of martyrs, who were faithful even unto death. . . .

Father, we thank Thee also for the unmentioned martyrs, for the glorious company of prophets whom history makes no written record of, but whose words and whose lives are garnered up in the great life of humanity. . . .

And for ourselves to whom Thou hast

given so many talents, and the opportunity so glorious for their use, we pray Thee that we may distinguish between the doctrines of men and Thine eternal commandments, and that no reverence to the old may blind our eyes to evils that have come down from other days, and no fondness for new things ever lead us to grasp the hidden evil when we take the specious good; but may we separate between the right and the wrong, and choose those things that are wise to direct, and profitable for our daily use. . . .

May we cultivate every noble faculty of our nature, and over all the humbler faculties may we enthrone the great commanding powers, which shall rule and regulate our life into order and strength and beauty, and fill our souls with the manifold delight of those who know Thee and serve Thee and love Thee with all their understanding and all their heart.

In the stern duties which are before us, Father in heaven, may Thy light burn clear in our tabernacle, and when Thou callest us may our lamps be trimmed and burning, our loins girt about, our feet readily sandalled for the road, and our souls prepared for Thee. Thus may Thy kingdom come, and Thy will be done on earth as it is in heaven. *Amen.*

LXII. Arise, O LORD, who judgest the earth; and as Thou dwellest in and possessest the faith of all nations, suffer us not to abide in darkness: and grant that we may not lay the foundations of our faith on the sand where the whirlwind may overthrow them, but be established on the rock which is steadfast in Thee. *Amen.*

# B. Collects of Ethical and Spiritual Religion

# B. Collects of Ethical and Spiritual Religion

LXIII. Bless our children, O God, and help us so to fashion their souls, by precept and by example, that they shall ever love the good, flee from sin, revere Thy word and honor Thy name. May they, planted in the house of the Lord, flourish in the courts of our God; may they guard for future ages the truths revealed to their forefathers. *Amen.*

LXIV. Almighty God, Thou hast graciously permitted us to awake to the light of a new day. Let us not sink into the darkness of error and sin. Do not withdraw Thy hand from us; let Thy love be near us. Incline our hearts unto Thee, that all our thoughts and words and deeds may make answer to the call of Thy will; that we may follow whither Thy word shall lead, and may ever do what is right and good in Thine eyes.

Grant us clear insight into the truth, steadfast apprehension of the right, that through the mazes of this world's errors and temptations we may walk unhindered and unfalteringly the pathway of godliness. Grant us strength to do Thy will. Lead Thou us by the hand, as a father leadeth his child, lest we fall.

Satisfy us early through Thy mercy, that we may rejoice in Thee and give thanks unto Thee all the days of our life. *Amen.*

LXV. O God the Father, . . . whose Name is great, whose nature is blissful, whose goodness is inexhaustible, Thou God and Master of all things, who art blessed forever; who sittest on the Cherubim, and art glorified by the Seraphim; before whom stand thousands of thousands and ten thousand times ten thousand, the hosts of holy Angels and Archangels; sanctify, O Lord, our souls and bodies and spirits, and touch our apprehensions and search out our consciences, and cast out of us every evil thought, every base desire, all envy and pride, and hypocrisy, all falsehood, all deceit, all worldly anxiety, all covetousness, vainglory and sloth, all malice, all wrath, all anger, all remembrance of injuries, all blasphemy, and every emotion of the flesh and spirit that is contrary to Thy holy will. And grant us, O LORD, the Lover of men, with freedom, without condemnation, with a pure heart and a contrite soul, without confusion of face and with sanctified lips, boldly to call upon Thee, our holy God and Father who art in heaven. *Amen.*

LXVI. LORD our God, great, eternal, wonderful in glory, who keepest covenant and promises for those that love Thee with their whole heart; who art the Life of all, the Help of those that flee unto Thee, the Hope of those who cry unto Thee; cleanse us from our sins, secret and open, and from every thought displeasing to Thy goodness — cleanse our bodies and souls, our hearts and consciences, that with a pure heart and a clear soul, with perfect love and calm hope, we may venture confidently and fearlessly to pray unto Thee. *Amen.*

LXVII. O God, Holy Ghost, Sanctifier of the faithful, visit, we pray thee, this Congregation with Thy love and favor; enlighten their minds more and more with the light of the everlasting Gospel; graft in their hearts a love of the truth; increase in them true religion; nourish them with all goodness; and of Thy great mercy keep them in the same, O blessed Spirit. . . . *Amen.*

LXVIII. O God, the Life of the faithful, the Bliss of the righteous, mercifully receive the prayers of Thy suppliants, that the souls which thirst for Thy promises may evermore be filled from Thine abundance. *Amen.*

LXIX. Shine into our hearts, O loving Master, by the pure light of the knowledge of Thyself; and open the eyes of our mind to the contemplation of Thy . . . teaching, and put into us the fear of Thy blessed commandments; that trampling down all carnal appetites, we may follow a spiritual life, thinking and doing all things according to Thy good pleasure. For Thou art our sanctification and our illumination, and to Thee we render glory, . . . now and ever, and unto ages of ages. *Amen.*

LXX. We beseech Thee, O LORD, in Thy loving-kindness, to pour Thy holy light into our souls; that we may ever be devoted to

Thee, by whose wisdom we were created, and by whose providence we are governed. . . . *Amen.*

LXXI. O God, who hast prepared for those who love Thee such good things as pass man's understanding; pour into our hearts such love toward Thee, that we, loving Thee above all things, may obtain Thy promises, which exceed all that we can desire. . . *Amen.*

LXXII. Lord of all power and might, who art the author and giver of all good things; graft in our hearts the love of Thy Name, increase in us true religion, nourish us with all goodness, and of Thy great mercy keep us in the same. . . . *Amen.*

LXXIII. Heavenly King, Paraclete, Spirit of Truth, who art everywhere present and fillest all things, the Treasury of good things and the Bestower of life, come and dwell in us, and purify us from every stain, and save our souls, in Thy goodness. *Amen.*

LXXIV. Abba, Father, fulfil the office of Thy Name towards Thy servants; do Thou govern, protect, preserve, sanctify, guide, console them; let them be so enkindled with love for Thee that they may not be despised by Thee, O most merciful LORD, most tender Father! *Amen.*

LXXV. Show the light of Thy countenance upon us, O LORD, that the going forth of Thy word may give light and understanding, to nourish the hearts of the simple; and that while our desire is set on Thy commandments, we may receive with open heart the Spirit of wisdom and understanding. *Amen.*

LXXVI. Almighty God, who seest that we have no power of ourselves to help ourselves; keep us both outwardly in our bodies, and inwardly in our souls; that we may be defended in our adversities which may happen to the body, and from all evil thoughts which may assault and hurt the soul. . . . *Amen.*

LXXVII. O God, with whom is the well of life, and in whose light we see light; increase in us, we beseech Thee, the brightness of divine knowledge, whereby we may be able to reach Thy plenteous fountain; impart to our thirsting souls the draught of life, and restore to our darkened minds the light from heaven. *Amen.*

LXXVIII. Be Thou, O Lord, our protection, who art our redemption; direct our minds by Thy gracious presence, and watch over our paths with guiding love; that among the snares which lie hidden in this path wherein we walk, we may so pass onward with hearts fixed on Thee, that by the track of faith we may come to be where Thou wouldst have us. *Amen.*

LXXIX. Grant Thy servants, O God, to be set on fire with Thy Spirit, strengthened by Thy power, illuminated by Thy splendor, filled with Thy grace, and to go forward by Thine aid. Give them, O Lord, a right faith, perfect love, true humility. Grant, O Lord, that there may be in us simple affection, brave patience, persevering obedience, perpetual peace, a pure mind, a right and clean heart, a good will, a holy conscience, spiritual compunction, ghostly strength, a life unspotted and unblamable; and after having manfully finished our course, may we be enabled happily to enter into Thy kingdom. *Amen.*

LXXX. Hear our prayers, O Lord, and consider our desires. Give unto us true humility, a meek and quiet spirit, a loving and a friendly, a holy and a useful manner of life; bearing the burdens of our neighbors, denying ourselves, and studying to benefit others, and to please Thee in all things. Grant us to be righteous in performing promises, loving to our relatives, careful of our charges; to be gentle and easy to be entreated, slow to anger, and readily prepared for every good work. *Amen.*

LXXXI. We offer up unto Thee our prayers and intercessions, for those especially who have in any matter hurt, grieved, or found fault with us, or who have done us any damage or displeasure.

For all those also whom, at any time, we may have vexed, troubled, burdened, and scandalized, by words or deeds, knowingly or in ignorance; that Thou wouldst grant us all equally pardon for our sins and for our offences against each other.

Take away from our hearts, O Lord, all suspiciousness, indignation, wrath, and contention, and whatsoever may hurt charity, and lessen brotherly love.

Have mercy, O Lord, have mercy on those that crave Thy mercy, give grace unto them that stand in need thereof, and make us such as that we may be worthy to enjoy Thy grace, and go forward to life eternal. *Amen.*

LXXXII. Almighty and everlasting God, by whose Spirit the whole body of the Church is governed and sanctified ; receive our supplications and prayers, which we offer before Thee for all estates of men in Thy holy Church, that every member of the same, in his vocation and ministry, may truly and godly serve Thee. . . . *Amen.*

LXXXIII. O God, of surpassing goodness, whom the round world with one voice doth praise for Thy sweet benignity ; we pray Thee to remove from us all error, that so we may perform Thy will. . . . *Amen.*

LXXXIV. O LORD, our hiding-place, grant us wisdom, we pray Thee, to seek no hiding-place out of Thee in life or in death. Now hide us in Thine own Presence, from the provoking of all men, and keep us from the strife of tongues. Make us meek, humble, patient, and teach us to seek peace and ensue it. *Amen.*

LXXXV. O LORD, grant all who contend for the faith, never to injure it by clamor and impatience; but, speaking Thy precious truth in love, so to present it that it may be loved, and that men may see in it Thy goodness and beauty. *Amen.*

LXXXVI. Grant us, O Lord, to pass this day in gladness and peace, without stumbling and without stain; that, reaching the eventide victorious over all temptation, we may praise Thee, the eternal God, who art blessed, and dost govern all things, world without end. *Amen.*

LXXXVII. Grant to us, Lord, we beseech Thee, the spirit to think and do always such things as are right; that we, who cannot do anything that is good without Thee, may by Thee be enabled to live according to Thy will. . . . *Amen.*

LXXXVIII. Almighty and everlasting God, give unto us the increase of faith, hope, and charity; and, that we may obtain that which Thou dost promise, make us to love that which Thou dost command. . . . *Amen.*

LXXXIX. Govern all by Thy wisdom, O Lord, so that our souls may always be serving Thee as Thou dost will, and not as we may choose. Do not punish us, we beseech Thee, by granting that which we wish or ask, if it offend Thy love, which would always live in us. Let us die to ourselves, that so we may serve Thee; let us live to Thee, who in Thyself art the true Life. *Amen.*

XC. O God, Thou art Life, Wisdom, Truth, Bounty, and Blessedness, the Eternal, the only true Good! Our God and our LORD, Thou art our hope and our heart's joy. We confess, with thanksgiving, that Thou hast made us in Thine image, that we may direct all our thoughts to Thee, and love Thee. LORD, make us to know Thee aright, that we may more and more love, and enjoy, and possess Thee. And since, in the life here below, we cannot fully attain this blessedness, let it at least grow in us day by day, until it all be fulfilled at last in the life to come. Here be the knowledge of Thee increased, and there let it be perfected. Here let our love to Thee grow, and there let it ripen; that our joy, being here great in hope, may there in fruition be made perfect. *Amen.*

XCI. O God . . . whose name is great, whose nature is blissful, whose goodness is inexhaustible, God and Ruler of all things, who art blessed forever; before whom stand thousands and thousands, and ten thousand times ten thousand, the hosts of holy angels and archangels; sanctify, O LORD, our souls and bodies and spirits, search our consciences, and cast out of us every evil thought, every base desire, all envy and pride, all wrath and anger, and all that is contrary to Thy holy will. And grant us, O LORD, Lover of men, with a pure heart and contrite soul, to call upon Thee, our holy God and Father who art in heaven. *Amen.*

XCII. O Almighty God, who alone canst order the unruly wills and affections of sinful men; grant unto Thy people, that they may love the thing which Thou commandest, and desire that which Thou dost promise; that so, among the sundry and manifold changes of the world, our hearts may surely there be fixed, where true joys are to be found. . . . *Amen.*

XCIII. O LORD, from whom all good things do come; grant to us, Thy humble servants, that by Thy holy inspiration we may think those things that are good, and by Thy merciful guiding may perform the same. . . . *Amen.*

XCIV. Hear us, O never-failing Light, LORD our God, the Fountain of Light, the Light of Thine Angels, Principalities, Powers, and of all intelligent beings; who hast created the light of Thy Saints. May our souls be lamps of Thine, kindled and illuminated by Thee. May they shine and burn with the truth, and never go out in darkness and ashes. May the gloom of sins be cleared away, and the light of perpetual faith abide within us. *Amen.*

XCV. O God of Light, Father of Life, Giver of Wisdom, Benefactor of our souls, who givest to the faint-hearted who put their trust in Thee those things into which the angels desire to look; O Sovereign LORD, who hast brought us up from the depths of darkness to Light, who hast given us life from death, who hast graciously bestowed upon us freedom from slavery, and who hast scattered the darkness of sin within us; do Thou now also enlighten the eyes of our understanding, and sanctify us wholly in soul, body, and spirit. *Amen.*

XCVI. O most dear and tender Father, our Defender and Nourisher; endue us with Thy grace, that we may cast off the great blindness of our minds, and carefulness of worldly things, and may put our whole study and care in keeping of Thy holy law; and that we may labor and travail for our necessities in this life, like the birds of the air and the lilies of the field, without care. For Thou hast promised to be careful for us; and hast commanded that upon Thee we should cast our care, who livest and reignest, world without end. *Amen.*

XCVII. Give strength, O LORD, to those who seek Thee, and continually pour into their souls the holy desire of seeking Thee; that they who long to see Thy face may not crave the world's pernicious pleasure. *Amen.*

XCVIII. Almighty and merciful God, who dost grant unto Thy faithful people the grace to make every path of life temporal the straight and narrow way which leadeth unto life eternal, grant that we, who know that we have no strength as of ourselves to help ourselves, and therefore do put all our trust in Thine almighty power, may, by the assistance of Thy heavenly grace, always prevail in all things, against whatsoever shall arise to fight against us. *Amen.*

XCIX. LORD, our God, great, eternal, wonderful in glory, who keepest covenant and promises for those that love Thee with their whole heart; who art the Life of all, the Help of those that flee unto Thee, the Hope of those who cry unto Thee; cleanse us from our sins, secret and open, and from every thought displeasing to Thy goodness — cleanse our bodies and souls, our hearts and consciences, that with a pure heart and a clear soul, with perfect love and calm hope, we may venture confidently and fearlessly to pray unto Thee. *Amen.*

C. O God, the Light of every heart that sees Thee, the Life of every soul that loves Thee, the Strength of every mind that seeks Thee, grant us ever to continue steadfast in Thy holy love. Be Thou the joy of our hearts; take them all to Thyself, and therein abide. The house of the soul is, we confess, too narrow for Thee; do Thou enlarge it, that Thou mayest enter in; it is ruinous, but do Thou repair it. It has that within which must offend Thine eyes; we confess and know it; but whose help shall we implore in cleansing it, but Thine alone? To Thee, therefore, we cry urgently, begging that Thou wilt cleanse us from our secret faults, and keep Thy servants from presumptuous sins, that they never get dominion over us. *Amen.*

CI. O Thou holy and unspeakable, Thou wonderful and mighty God, whose power and wisdom hath no end, before whom all powers tremble, at whose glance the heavens and the earth flee away, Thou art Love, Thou art our Father, and we will love and worship Thee forever and ever! Thou hast deigned to show pity on us, and a ray from Thy light hath shone upon our inward eye. Guide us on into the perfect light, that it may illumine us wholly, and that all darkness may flee away. Let the holy flame of Thy love so burn in our hearts that they be made pure and we may see Thee, O God; for it is the pure in heart who see Thee. Thou hast set us free; Thou hast drawn us to Thee; therefore forsake us not, but keep us always in Thy grace. Guide us and rule us, and perfect us for Thy kingdom. *Amen.*

CII. O LORD, we beseech Thee, absolve Thy people from their offences; that through

Thy bountiful goodness we may all be delivered from the bands of those sins, which by our frailty we have committed. . . . *Amen.*

CIII. O Everlasting God, who hast ordained and constituted the services of angels and men in a wonderful order; mercifully grant that, as Thy holy angels always do Thee service in heaven, so, by Thy appointment, they may succor and defend us on earth. . . . *Amen.*

CIV. LORD God Almighty, who art our true Peace, and Love eternal, enlighten our souls with the brightness of Thy peace, and purify our consciences with the sweetness of Thy love, that we may with peaceful hearts wait for the Author of peace, and in the adversities of this world may ever have Thee for our Guardian and Protector; and so being fenced about by Thy care, may heartily give ourselves to the love of Thy peace. *Amen.*

CV. O Thou, who art the true Sun of the world, evermore rising, and never going down; who, by Thy most wholesome appearing and sight dost nourish and make joyful all things, as well that are in heaven, as also that are on earth; we beseech Thee mercifully and favorably to shine into our hearts, that the night and darkness of sin, and the mists of error on every side, being driven away, Thou brightly shining within our hearts, we may all our life long go without any stumbling or offence, and may walk as in the day-time, being pure and clean from the works of darkness, and abounding in all good works which Thou hast prepared for us to walk in. *Amen.*

CVI. We beseech Thee, O LORD, to renew Thy people inwardly and outwardly, that as Thou wouldst not have them to be hindered by bodily pleasures, Thou mayest make them vigorous with spiritual purpose; and refresh them in such sort by things transitory, that Thou mayest grant them rather to cleave to things eternal. *Amen.*

CVII. O Almighty God, who hast knit together Thine elect in one communion and fellowship, grant us grace so to follow thy blessed saints in all virtuous and godly living, that we may come to those unspeakable joys which Thou hast prepared for those who unfeignedly love Thee. *Amen.*

CVIII. Almighty God, unto whom all hearts are open, all desires known, and from whom no secrets are hid, cleanse the thoughts of our hearts by the inspiration of Thy Holy Spirit, that we may perfectly love Thee, and worthily magnify Thy holy name. . . . *Amen.*

CIX. O Almighty God, grant, we beseech Thee, that we whose trust is under the shadow of Thy wings may, through the help of Thy power, overcome all evils that rise up against us. *Amen.*

CX. Bestow Thy light upon us, O LORD, so that, being rid of the darkness of our hearts, we may attain unto the true light. *Amen.*

CXI. O God, who hast in mercy taught us how good it is to follow the holy desires which Thou manifoldly puttest into our hearts, and how bitter is the grief of falling short of whatever beauty our minds behold, strengthen us, we beseech Thee, to walk steadfastly throughout life in the better path which our hearts once chose ; and give us wisdom to tread it prudently in Thy fear, as well as cheerfully in Thy love ; so that, having been faithful to Thee all the days of our life here, we may be able hopefully to resign ourselves into Thy hands hereafter. *Amen.*

CXII. LORD, we beseech Thee, grant Thy people grace to withstand the temptations of the world, the flesh, and the devil; and with pure hearts and minds to follow Thee, the only God. *Amen.*

CXIII. Grant, we beseech Thee, merciful LORD, to Thy faithful people pardon and peace, that they may be cleansed from all their sins and serve Thee with a quiet mind. *Amen.*

CXIV. Grant, we beseech Thee, O LORD God, unto all Thy servants, that they may continually enjoy health both of mind and body, may be delivered from the present sadness, and enter into the joy of Thine eternal gladness. *Amen.*

CXV. Blessed are all Thy saints, our God and King, who have travelled over the tempestuous sea of mortality, and have at last made the desired port of peace and felicity. Oh, cast a gracious eye upon us who are still in our dangerous voyage. Remember and succor us in our distress, and think on them that lie exposed to the rough storms of troubles and temptations. Strengthen our weakness, that we may do valiantly in this spiritual war; help us against our own negligence and cowardice, and defend us from the treachery of our unfaithful hearts. Grant, O Lord, that we may bring our vessel safe to shore, unto our desired haven. *Amen.*

CXVI. Lord, we beseech Thee, pour on Thy servants the increase of faith, hope, and charity, that as they glory in knowing Thee as Lord they may by Thy governance not feel the sorrows of this world; but both faithfully serve Thee in time, and enjoy Thee in eternity. *Amen.*

CXVII. From untruth lead us, O Lord, to Thy truth; from darkness, O Spirit, lead us to Thy light; from death, O Eternal, lead us to Thy eternal life. Thou Awful One, let Thy countenance shine upon us in love, and do Thou keep us from all harm and danger. *Peace!*

CXVIII. O God, who canst save by obedience of the spirit, men lost by weakness of the flesh, grant us so to have our inward sight quickened, and our better mind strengthened, that we may avoid what destroys us, and lay hold on what works perpetual peace. *Amen.*

CXIX. We entreat Thy mercy with our whole heart, that, as Thou defendest us against things adverse to the body, so Thou wilt set us free from the enemies of the soul; and, as Thou grantest to us to rejoice in outward tranquillity, so vouchsafe to us Thine inward peace. *Amen.*

CXX. Eternal God, who by Thy holy breath of power makest us a new creation for Thyself, we beseech Thee to preserve what Thou hast created, and consecrate what Thou hast cleansed; that by Thy grace we may be found in that form, the thought of which ever dwells with Thee, and which Thou willest fulfilled in man. *Amen.*

CXXI. O God, who hast enkindled in the holy bosoms of all Thy saints so great an ardor of faith that they despised all bodily pains, while hastening with all earnestness to Thee, the Author of life; hear our prayers, and grant that the hateful sweetness of sin may wax faint in us, and we may glow with the infused warmth of love for Thee; through Thy mercy, O our God, who art blessed, and dost live, and govern all things, world without end. *Amen.*

CXXII. O God, in whose sight to sin is to die, but in whose knowledge is life, and Thy service perfect freedom, grant that as by necessity of nature we have borne the likeness of things earthly, so by inward transformation of Thy Spirit we may attain to things heavenly, and dwell in Thy likeness forever. *Amen.*

CXXIII. Infinite Ruler of creation, whose Spirit dwells in every world! we look not into the solemn heavens for Thee, though Thou art there; we search not in the ocean for Thy presence, though it murmurs with Thy voice; we wait not for the wings of the wind to bring Thee nigh, though they are Thy messengers; for Thou art in our hearts, O God, and makest Thine abode in the deep places of our thought and love; and into each gentle affection, each contrite sorrow, each higher aspiration we would retire to meet and worship Thee. *Amen.*

CXXIV. O Thou Wisdom of God, the living Word and everlasting Power of the

Father, who camest forth out of the goodness of the Eternal Will, and showest the unspeakable depth of the Divine Majesty; without Thee is nothing, but by Thee are all things, and in Thee alone all things stand fast; Thou art God coming forth from God, for of Thy creative will we are what we are: Grant that Thy love may prevail over our unworthiness, and Thy promise be stronger than our faithlessness; so let Thy providence be our deliverance, and Thy grace our life, and Thy Truth our healing, that our weakness being filled with Thy strength, we may by Thy gift be lifted up to the Father, with whom Thou livest and art one forever. *Amen.*

CXXV. Hear us, O never-failing Light, LORD our God, our only Light, the Fountain of light, the Light of Thine Angels, Thrones, Dominions, Principalities, Powers, and of all intelligent beings; who hast created the light of Thy saints. May our souls be lamps of Thine, kindled and illuminated by Thee. May they shine and burn with the truth, and never go out in darkness and ashes. May we be Thy house, shining from Thee, shining in Thee; may we shine and fail not; may we ever worship Thee; in Thee may we be kindled, and not be extinguished. Being filled with Thy splendor, . . . may we shine forth inwardly; may the gloom of sins be cleared away, and the light of perpetual faith abide within us. *Amen.*

CXXVI. Thou Good Omnipotent, who so carest for every one of us, as if Thou caredst for him alone; and so for all, as if all were but one! Blessed is the man who loveth Thee, and his friend in Thee, and his enemy for Thee. For he only loses none dear to him, to whom all are dear in Him who cannot be lost. And who is that but our God, the God that made heaven and earth, and filleth them, even by filling them creating them? And Thy law is truth, and truth is Thyself. We behold how some things pass away that others may replace them, but Thou dost never depart, O God, our Father supremely good, Beauty of all things beautiful. To Thee will we intrust whatsoever we have received from Thee; so shall we lose nothing. Thou madest us for Thyself, and our hearts are restless until they repose in Thee. *Amen.*

CXXVII. Almighty and everlasting God,

whose power is unchangeable and light eternal, mercifully regard the wonderful mystery of Thy whole Church, and silently work the work of human salvation by Thine unchanging purpose, until the whole world shall experience and see the downcast raised, the decayed renewed, and all things returned to their perfection, by the might of that Spirit from whom they took their beginning. . . . *Amen.*

CXXVIII. LORD, let the blood of all those who have striven for right, and died for truth, be ever precious before Thee; and let not the sufferings which our mothers bore for us, nor the sighing of those who have prayed for us, nor the striving of those who have taught, or any way helped us, or pleaded for our cause, come to nought, or fail of good fruit forever. *Amen.*

CXXIX. O LORD, strip from us the sophistries of self-seeking, of vain custom, of earthly pride and fear; and set free our minds for the reverence of all grace and truth, our hearts for the love of whatever things are pure and good, and our wills for faithful accord with Thine. *Amen.*

CXXX. O God, the Life of the faithful, the Joy of the righteous, mercifully receive the prayers of Thy suppliants, that the souls which thirst for Thy promises may evermore be filled from Thine abundance, to the glory of Thy holy Name. *Amen.*

CXXXI. Enlarge our souls, O LORD, with a divine charity, that we may hope all things, believe all things, endure all things, and become messengers of Thy healing mercy to the grievances and infirmities of men. *Amen.*

CXXXII. O God, who dwellest in the Holy Place, and forsakest not pious hearts, deliver us from earthly desire and unruly appetite; that no sin may reign in us; but that we may with free spirits serve Thee, our only Lord, whose name is Holy, Holy, Holy. *Amen.*

CXXXIII. God of all power and might! Thy secret place shall be our shelter still. On one thing our heart is fixed, that we will put our trust in Thee, though terrors also are around Thee. Thou hangest the world upon nothing: yet we dwell thereon in peace. Thou barest Thine arm in the lightning: yet we work in the fields which Thou smitest, and own it as the messenger of Thy perfect will. Darkness and tempest are often round Thee; yet we expect Thy light behind every cloud.

But, O God most just! let not our security be the confidence of fools. Never may our blind hearts say, "How doth God know? the heavens are covered that He seeth not"; but always may we lie open to Thy living presence, and in the silence of the night, when deep sleep falleth upon man, feel the passing of Thy Spirit and say "We are not alone, for the Father is with us." Only on Thy tender mercy can we rest. When we look up to Thee, we dare ask for no recompense for obedience, lest we receive only the wages of sin, and die: but we leave ourselves to Thine infinite pity, in the hope that to them that have loved much and repented with many tears, Thou wilt say, "Your sins are forgiven; go in peace." *Amen.*

CXXXIV. Merciful LORD, who gavest the martyrs of our own country such faithfulness, that they yielded their bodies to be burnt in the flame, for the freedom of men's souls; grant that the candle which they lighted may never be quenched in our land; but enable us, when Thou shalt call us, to leave, if need be, what we have held dear, and with undaunted faith to follow Thee, our Saviour, and true refuge of our souls. *Amen.*

CXXXV. O Thou in whom we live and move and have our being! who hast created and known us, one by one! All generations shall worship Thee, while sun and moon endure. Thine we must needs be: if Thou but look for us, we are; and if Thou but hide Thy face, Thou prevailest against us, and we pass away.

In our idle words, we forget Thy listening ear; in our time of wealth, Thy watch upon our trust; in the world's vain show, Thy great reality; and in our anxious troubles, Thy waiting to bear the burden for us.

O Thou Everlasting Hope of men! Why should we deem Thee a stranger upon the earth, as a wayfarer that tarrieth for a night and turneth aside? Thou art yet in the midst, if we but seek Thee with an open soul. May we begin anew to do Thy will, that we may know Thee as the Living God; renouncing every low desire which may turn the light that is within us to darkness, and surrendering ourselves to that love of what is pure and true, by which we become children of the Highest. In malice, may we be as infants; in understanding, as men; in truth, as the martyrs; in affection, as the angels.

We yield ourselves to Thee. We will be afraid of neither sorrow nor death in a world where many saintly souls have sanctified them by a divine patience, and amid a Providence wherein no evil thing can dwell. Clinging unto Thee, we shall not perish with the fashion of this world that passeth away. . . . In Thee, O LORD, is our undying trust. *Amen.*

CXXXVI. O Spirit of grace, who withholdest Thy blessing from none! take from us the tediousness and anxiety of a selfish mind, the unfruitfulness of cold affections, the weakness of an inconstant will. With the simplicity of a great purpose, the quiet of a meek temper, and the power of a well-ordered soul, may we pass through the toils and watches of our pilgrimage; grateful for all that may render the burden of duty light; and even in strong trouble rejoicing to be deemed worthy of the severer service of Thy will. *Amen.*

CXXXVII. Father of all mercy and truth, by whom the meek are guided in judgment, and light riseth in darkness unto them that turn to Thee; grant us in all doubts and uncertainties the grace to ask what Thou wouldst have us to do; that the spirit of wisdom may save us from all false choices; that in Thy light we may see light, and in Thy straight path may never stumble. *Amen.*

CXXXVIII. We beseech Thee, O LORD, let our hearts be graciously enlightened by Thy holy radiance, that we may serve Thee without fear in holiness and righteousness all the days of our life; that so we may escape the darkness of this world, and by Thy guidance attain the land of eternal brightness; through Thy mercy, O blessed LORD, who dost live and govern all things, world without end. *Amen.*

CXXXIX. Grant, we beseech Thee, Almighty God, unto us who know that we are weak, and who trust in Thee because we know that Thou art strong, the gladsome help of Thy loving-kindness, both here in time and hereafter in eternity. *Amen.*

CXL. O LORD, we beseech Thee that

Thy people may grow ever in love toward Thee, their Father who art in heaven, and may be so schooled by holy works, that ever, as Thou dost pour Thy gifts upon them, they may walk before Thee in all such things as be well pleasing in the sight of Thy Divine Majesty. *Amen.*

CXLI. We bless and praise and magnify Thee, O God of our fathers, who hast led us out of the shadows of night once more into the light of day. Unto Thy loving-kindness we make our entreaty; be merciful to our misdeeds; accept our prayers in the fulness of Thy compassion, for Thou art our refuge from one generation to another, O merciful and Almighty God. Suffer the true Sun of Thy righteousness to shine in our hearts, enlighten our reason, and purify our senses; that so we may walk honestly as in the day, in the way of Thy commandments, and reach at last the life eternal. For Thou art the Fountain of Life, and in Thy light shall we see light. *Amen.*

CXLII. Almighty God, of Thy fulness grant unto us who need so much, who lack so much, who have so little, wisdom and strength. Bring our wills unto Thine. Lift our understandings into Thy heavenly light; that we thereby beholding those things which are right, and being drawn by Thy love, may bring our will and our understanding together to Thy service; until at last, body and soul and spirit may be all Thine, and Thou be our Father and our Eternal Friend. *Amen.*

CXLIII. O Thou who art Love and dwellest in love! teach us herein to be followers of Thee, as dear children. Never may we shut our hearts against the sorrows of even the unthankful and the evil. Make us organs of Thy tender mercy, to soothe the wretched, to lift the penitent, to seek and to save the lost; till all shall at length know themselves Thy children, and be one with each other and with Thee. *Amen.*

CXLIV. O God, who art Thyself the exceeding great Reward of all faithful souls, grant unto us to advance daily to the utmost of our power in godliness, so that we, seeking ever that which is more perfect, may happily attain unto Thine everlasting glory. *Amen.*

CXLV. O most merciful and gracious God,

we beseech Thee to hear our prayers, and to deliver our hearts from the temptation of evil thoughts, that by Thy goodness, we may become a fitting habitation for Thy Holy Spirit. *Amen.*

CXLVI. O LORD, because being compassed with infirmities we oftentimes sin and ask pardon, help us to forgive as we would be forgiven; neither mentioning old offences committed against us, nor dwelling upon them in thought, nor being influenced by them in heart; but loving our brother freely as Thou freely lovest us. *Amen.*

CXLVII. Almighty God, who hast caused the light of eternal life to shine upon the world, we beseech Thee that our hearts may be so kindled with heavenly desires, and Thy love so shed abroad in us by Thy Holy Spirit, that we may continually seek the things which are above; and, abiding in purity of heart and mind, may at length attain unto Thine everlasting kingdom. *Amen.*

CXLVIII. O God, who makest all things work together for good to them that love Thee, pour into our hearts such steadfast love to

Thee that those desires which spring from Thee may not be turned aside by any temptation. *Amen.*

CXLIX. O God, who dost incline the hearts of all Thy true people that they should mind the same things and be at peace among themselves, grant, we beseech Thee, that we may so love what Thou commandest, and so desire what Thou dost promise, that amid the sundry and manifold changes of this world our hearts may remain fixed, resting in Thee, till we attain at length to Thy presence, where is fulness of joy. . . . *Amen.*

CL. Grant, we beseech Thee, O LORD, the Giver and Guide of all reason, that we may always be mindful of the nature, of the dignity, and of the privileges Thou hast honored us with; that we act in all things as becomes free agents, to the subduing and governing of our passions, to the refining them from flesh and sense, and to the rendering them subservient to excellent purposes. Grant us also Thy favorable assistance in the forming and directing our judgment, and enlighten us with Thy truth, that we may discern those things which are really good, and, having discovered them, may love and cleave steadfastly to the same. And, finally, disperse, we pray Thee, those mists which darken the eyes of our mind, that so we may have a perfect understanding, and know both God and man, and what to each is due. *Amen.*

CLI. LORD God, of might inconceivable, of glory incomprehensible, of mercy immeasurable, of benignity ineffable; do Thou, O Master, look down upon us in Thy tender love, and show forth, towards us and those who pray with us, Thy rich mercies and compassions. *Amen.*

CLII. Kindle in our hearts, O Divine Master and Lover of men, the pure light of Thy divine knowledge, and open the eyes of our minds to the understanding of Thy Gospel. Plant in us the fear of Thy blessed commandments, that, trampling upon all selfish and sinful desires, we may attain to spiritual life, both thinking and doing all things according to Thy Word. For Thou art the illumination of our souls, and to Thee we ascribe the glory forever. *Amen.*

CLIII. O merciful God, grant that we may covet earnestly, with an ardent mind, those things which please Thee; that we may search them wisely, know them truly, and fulfil them perfectly, to the praise and glory of Thy holy Name. May we rejoice in nothing but in that which moveth us to Thee, and be sorry for nothing but for that which draweth us from Thee; desiring to please none, nor fearing to displease any beside Thee. O God, let us be humble without pretence, cheerful without lightness, sober without dulness, trusting without presumption, and fearing without despair. Grant us understanding to know Thee, diligence to seek Thee, wisdom to find Thee, patience to wait for Thee, and hope to embrace Thee; and in heaven through Thy grace to enjoy Thy joys and Thy rewards forever. *Amen.*

CLIV. O God, whose days are without end, and whose mercies cannot be numbered; make us, we beseech Thee, deeply sensible of the shortness and uncertainty of human life; and let thy Holy Spirit lead us through this vale of misery, in holiness and righteousness, all the days of our lives; that, when we shall have served Thee in our generation, we may be gathered unto our fathers, having the testimony of a good conscience; in the communion of the catholic Church; in the confidence of a certain faith; in the comfort of a reasonable, religious, and holy hope; in favor with Thee, our God, and in perfect charity with the world. *Amen.*

CLV. Almighty God, with whom do live the spirits of those who depart hence in the Lord, and with whom the souls of the faithful, after they are delivered from the burden of the flesh, are in joy and felicity; we give Thee hearty thanks for the good examples of all those Thy servants who, having finished their course in faith, do now rest from their labors. And we beseech Thee that we, with all those who are departed in the true faith of thy holy Name, may have our perfect consummation and bliss, both in body and soul, in Thy eternal and everlasting glory. *Amen.*

# C. Collects of Religion—Society and the State

# C. Collects of Religion—Society and the State

CLVI. We, therefore, beseech Thee, O our God, to help us banish from our hearts all pride and vainglory, all confidence in worldly possessions, all self-sufficient leaning on our own reason. Fill us with the spirit of meekness, and the grace of modesty, that we may become wise in Thy fear. May we never forget that all we have and prize is but lent to us, a trust of which we must render an account to Thee. We beseech Thee, O heavenly Father, to put into our hearts the love and fear of Thee, that we may consecrate our lives to Thy service and glorify Thy name in the eyes of all peoples. *Amen.*

CLVII. Be with all men and women who spend themselves for the good of mankind and bear the burdens of others; who break bread to the hungry, clothe the naked, and take the friendless to their habitation. Establish Thou, O God, the works of their hands and grant them an abundant harvest of the good seed they are sowing. *Amen.*

CLVIII. Almighty God, who in former time leddest our fathers forth into a wealthy place, and didst set their feet in a large room, give Thy grace, we humbly beseech Thee, to us their children, that we may always approve ourselves a people mindful of Thy favors and glad to do Thy will. Bless our land with honorable industry, sound learning, and pure manners. Defend our liberties; preserve our unity. Save us from violence, discord, and confusion, from pride and arrogance, and from every evil way. Fashion into one happy people the multitude brought hither out of many kindreds and tongues. Endue with the spirit of wisdom those whom we intrust in Thy name with the authority of governance, to the end that there may be peace at home, and that we keep our place among the nations of the earth. In the time of our prosperity, temper our self-confidence with thankfulness, and in the day of trouble, suffer not our trust in Thee to fail. *Amen.*

CLIX. Albeit whatsoever is born of flesh is flesh, . . . so that no child of Adam hath any cause to boast himself of his birth and blood, seeing we have all one flesh and one blood ; . . . yet forasmuch as some by their wisdom, godliness, virtue, valiantness, strength, eloquence, learning, and policy be advanced above the common sort of people unto dignities and temporal promotions, as men worthy to have superiority in a commonwealth, and by this means have obtained among the people a more noble and worthy name ; we most earnestly beseech Thee from whom alone cometh the true nobility to so many as are born of Thee and made Thy sons through faith, whether they be rich or poor, noble or unnoble, to give a good spirit to our superiors, that as they be called gentlemen in name, so they may show themselves in all their doings, gentle, courteous, loving, pitiful, and liberal unto their inferiors ; living among them as natural fathers among their children, not polling, pilling, and oppressing them, but favoring, helping, and cherishing them ; not destroyers, but fathers of the commonalty ; not enemies to the poor, but aiders, helpers, and comforters of them : that when Thou shalt call them from this vale of wretchedness, they afore showing gentleness to the common people, may receive gentleness again at Thy merciful hand, even everlasting life. *Amen.*

λ   CLX. The earth is Thine, O Lord, and all that is contained therein; notwithstanding Thou hast given the possession thereof unto the children of men. We heartily pray Thee to send Thy Holy Spirit into the hearts of them that possess the grounds, pastures, and dwelling-places of the earth, that they, remembering themselves to be Thy tenants, may not rack and stretch out the rents of their houses and lands; nor yet take unreasonable fines and incomes, after the manner of covetous worldlings, but so let them out to others that the inhabitants thereof may both be able to pay the rents, and also honestly to live, to nourish their families, and to relieve the poor; give them grace also to consider that they are but strangers and pilgrims in this world, having here no dwelling-place, but seeking one to come; that they, remembering the short continuance of their life, may be content with that which is sufficient, and not join house to house, nor couple land to land, to the impoverishment of others, but so behave themselves in letting out their tenements, lands, and pastures, that after this life they may be received into everlasting dwelling-places. . . . *Amen.*

CLXI. Father of men, who regardest Thy children with compassion! Behold this earth, which Thou hast given to our care, hath many griefs, and is sad with a weight of shameful sins. Keep us pure from the evil, and make us strong to contend against it. Let us not shut our hearts against pity, O Thou All-merciful! but seek to heal the wounds with which our fellowmen lie stricken on the way. May we make no peace with oppression; but, amid the negligence of the world and the seduction of guilty custom, put into us the spirit of the holy prophets and martyrs of old, that we may cry aloud and spare not. Yet, O LORD, may it be that we sin not in our anger. Touch us with Thy gentleness; and so lift up within us a meek aspiring mind, that we may never say to our brother—"I am holier than thou," but only ask of Thee—"God, be merciful to me a sinner!" So may we labor and watch and pray for the coming of Thy kingdom. *Amen.*

CLXII. LORD of all, whose balance trieth the nations, to lift up or to cast down; Thou hast planted us, as a people, in quiet resting-places, and stretched out our branches over the sea, and laid upon us a mighty trust. Never through vain conceit may we be blind to the unchanging conditions of Thy blessing. The world and its fulness are Thine: our portion thereof may we hold, not in wanton self-will, but reverently, as of Thee; making it the stronghold of right, the refuge of the oppressed, and the moderator of lawless ambition. . . . Make all who speak or act for this nation true organs of Thine equity, that through their wisdom and faithfulness Thou mayest be our Lawgiver and Judge. And let it be that, as with the people so with the chiefs, as with the servants so with the master, as with the buyer so with the seller, all may know Thee as weighing the path of the just; that righteousness may be the girdle of our power. *Amen.*

CLXIII. Almighty LORD, of whose righteous will all things are, and were created; who liftest the islands out of the deep, and preparest not in vain the habitable world; Thou hast gathered our people into a great nation, and sent them to sow beside all waters, and multiply sure dwellings on the earth. Deepen the root of our life in everlasting righteousness ; and let not the crown of our pride be as a fading flower. Make us equal to our high trusts; reverent in the use of freedom, just in the exercise of power, generous in the protection of weakness. . . . To our Legislators and Counsellors give insight and faithfulness, that our laws may clearly speak the right, and our Judges purely interpret it. Let it be known among us how thou hatest robbery for burnt-offering ; that the gains of industry may be all upright, and the use of wealth considerate. May wisdom and knowledge be the stability of our times : and our deepest trust be in Thee, the Lord of nations and the King of kings. *Amen.*

## D. Doxologies and Benedictions

## D. Doxologies and Benedictions

CLXIV. Now unto the King, Eternal, Immortal, Invisible, the only wise God, be honor and glory forever and ever. *Amen.*

CLXV. Now unto Him that is able to keep us from falling, and to present us faultless before the presence of His glory with exceeding joy, to the only wise God our Saviour, be glory and majesty, dominion and power, both now and ever. *Amen.*

CLXVI. The Lord bless you and keep you : the Lord cause His face to shine upon you, and be gracious unto you : the Lord lift up ~~the light of~~ His countenance upon you, and give you peace. *Amen.*

# III

# Hymns

*A. Hymns of Universality*

# III

## Hymns

### A. Hymns of Universality

**I**                                     8. 8. 7.

1 One and universal Father,
   Here in rev'rent thought we gather,
     Seeking light in honoring Thee;
   Free our souls from error's fetter;
   Make us wiser, make us better;
     Be our guide, our guardian be!

2 For the truths of life to win us,
   Thou, O God, didst plant within us
     Aspirations high and bright;
   Bring us to Thy presence nearer,
   Let us see Thy glories clearer,
     When all mists shall melt in light.

**2**  L. M.

1 O Holy Ghost, Thou God of peace,
   Pity Thy Church, now rent in twain;
  Bid wrath, and strife, and variance cease,
   And let us all be one again;

2 One with our brethren here in love,
   And one with saints that are at rest,
  And one with angel hosts above,
   And one with God forever blest.

3 Oh, make on earth all churches one,
   One with the blessèd gone before,
  All knit in sweet communion,
   To love Thee, worship, and adore.

4 For one the Lord on whom we call,
   The Spirit one whom He hath given,
  One God and Father of us all,
   One Faith on earth, one Hope of Heaven.

**3**  C. M.

1 Immortal Love, forever full,
   Forever flowing free,
  Forever shared, forever whole,
   A never-ebbing sea;

2 Our outward lips confess the name
   All other names above;

    But love alone knows whence it came,
      And comprehendeth love.

3 Blow, winds of God, awake and blow
    The mists of earth away;
  Shine out, O Light divine, and show
    How wide and far we stray.

4 The letter fails, the systems fall,
    And every symbol wanes:
  The Spirit over-brooding all,
    Eternal Love, remains.


## 4                     8. 7.

1 God of ages and of nations,
    Every race and every time
  Hath received Thine inspirations,
    Glimpses of Thy truth sublime.
Ever spirits, in rapt vision,
    Passed the heavenly vale within;
Ever hearts, bowed in contrition,
    Found salvation from their sin.

2 Reason's noble aspiration,
    Truth in growing clearness saw;
Conscience spoke its condemnation,
    Or proclaimed the Eternal Law.

While Thine inward revelations
  Told Thy saints their prayers were heard,
Prophets to the guilty nations
  Spoke Thine everlasting word.

3 Lord, that word abideth ever;
   Revelation is not sealed;
  Answering unto man's endeavor,
   Truth and Right are still revealed.
  That which came to ancient sages,
   Greek, Barbarian, Roman, Jew,
  Written in the heart's deep pages,
   Shines to-day, forever new.

5                                         L. M.
1 Wherever through the ages rise
  The altars of self-sacrifice,
  Where love its arms hath opened wide,
  Or man for man has calmly died,

2 We see the same white wings outspread
  That hovered o'er the Master's head;
  And in all lands beneath the sun
  The heart affirmeth, Love is one.

3 Up from undated time they come,
  The martyr-souls of heathendom,

And to His cross and passion bring
Their fellowship of suffering.

4 And the great marvel of their death
To the one order witnesseth—
Each, in his measure, but a part
Of Thy unmeasured Over-Heart.

## 6     C. M.

1 City of God, how broad and far
    Outspread thy walls sublime!
The true thy chartered freemen are,
    Of every age and clime.

2 One holy Church, one army strong,
    One steadfast, high intent,
One faith and work, one hope and song,
    One King Omnipotent!

3 How purely hath thy speech come down
    From man's primeval youth!
And slow and vast thine empire grown
    Of Freedom, Love, and Truth!

4 The watch-fires gleam from night to night,
    With never-fainting ray;
Thy towers uprise, serene and bright,
    To meet the dawning day.

5 In vain the surges' angry shock,
   In vain the drifting sands ;
Unharmed, upon the Eternal Rock,
   The Eternal City stands !

## 7
C. M.

1 One holy Church of God appears
   Through every age and race,
Unwasted by the lapse of years,
   Unchanged by changing place.

2 From oldest time, on farthest shores,
   Beneath the pine or palm,
One Unseen Presence she adores,
   With silence or with psalm.

3 Her priests are all God's faithful sons,
   To serve the world raised up ;
The pure in heart her baptized ones ;
   Love, her communion-cup.

4 The truth is her prophetic gift,
   The soul her sacred page ;
And feet on mercy's errands swift
   Do make her pilgrimage.

5 O living Church, thine errand speed ;
   Fulfil thy task sublime ;
With bread of life earth's hunger feed ;
   Redeem the evil time !

## 8
8. 7.

1 We believe in Human Kindness
    Large amid the sons of men,
Nobler far in willing blindness
    Than in censure's keenest ken.
We believe in Self-Denial,
    And its secret throb of joy;
In the love that lives through trial,
    Dying not, though death destroy.

2 We believe in dreams of Duty,
    Warning us to self-control,—
Foregleams of the glorious beauty
    That shall yet transform the soul:
In the godlike wreck of nature
    Sin doth in the sinner leave,
That he may regain the stature
    He hath lost—we do believe.

3 We believe in Love renewing
    All that sin hath swept away,
Leaven-like its work pursuing
    Night by night and day by day:
In the power of its remoulding,
    In the grace of its reprieve,
In the glory of beholding
    Its perfection—we believe.

4 We believe in Love Eternal,
    Fixed in God's unchanging will,
That, beneath the deep infernal,
    Hath a depth that 's deeper still !
In its patience, its endurance
    To forbear and to retrieve,
In the large and full assurance
    Of its triumph—we believe.

## 9      L. M.

1 No human eyes Thy face may see ;
    No human thought Thy form may know ;
But all creation dwells in Thee,
    And Thy great life through all doth flow ;

2 And yet, oh strange and wondrous thought !
    Thou art a God who hearest prayer,
And every heart with sorrow fraught
    To seek Thy present aid may dare.

3 And though most weak our efforts seem
    Into one creed these thoughts to bind,
And vain the intellectual dream,
    To see and know th' Eternal Mind ;

4 Yet Thou wilt turn them not aside
    Who cannot solve Thy life divine,
But would give up all reason's pride
    To know their hearts approved by Thine.

5 So though we faint on life's dark hill,
    And thought grow weak and knowledge flee,
  Yet faith shall teach us courage still,
    And love shall guide us on to Thee.

**10**                                              L. M.

1 O Life that maketh all things new,
    The blooming earth, the thoughts of men!
  Our pilgrim feet, wet with thy dew,
    In gladness hither turn again.

2 From hand to hand the greeting flows,
    From eye to eye the signals run,
  From heart to heart the bright hope glows;
    The seekers of the Light are one;

3 One in the freedom of the Truth,
    One in the joy of paths untrod,
  One in the soul's perennial youth,
    One in the larger thought of God;

4 The freer step, the fuller breath,
    The wide horizon's grander view,
  The sense of life that knows no death,
    The Life that maketh all things new.

**11**                                             L. M.

1 O Love Divine, whose constant beam
    Shines on the eyes that will not see,

    And waits to bless us while we dream
        Thou leav'st us when we turn from Thee!

2 All souls that struggle and aspire,
    All hearts of prayer, by Thee are lit;
  And, dim or clear, Thy tongues of fire
    On dusky tribes and centuries sit.

3 Nor bounds, nor clime, nor creed Thou
    know'st:
  Wide as our need Thy favors fall;
  The white wings of the Holy Ghost
    Stoop, unseen, o'er the heads of all.

**12**                                                                   6s.

1 O thou not made with hands,
    Not throned above the skies,
  Nor walled with shining walls,
    Nor framed with stones of price,
  More bright than gold or gem,
    God's own Jerusalem!

2 Where'er the gentle heart
    Finds courage from above;
  Where'er the heart forsook
    Warms with the breath of love;
  Where faith bids fear depart,
    City of God! thou art.

3 Thou art where'er the proud
    In humbleness melts down;
Where self itself yields up;
    Where martyrs win their crown;
Where faithful souls possess
    Themselves in perfect peace.

4 Where in life's common ways
    With cheerful feet we go;
Where in His steps we tread
    Who trod the way of woe;
Where He is in the heart,
    City of God! thou art.

**13**    C. M.

1 From heart to heart, from creed to creed,
    The hidden river runs;
It quickens all the ages down,
    It binds the sires to sons,—
The stream of Faith, whose source is God,
    Whose sound, the sound of prayer,
Whose meadows are the holy lives
    Upspringing everywhere.

2 How deep it flowed in olden time,
    When men by it were strong
To dare the untrod wilderness,
    Charmed on by river-song!

Where'er they passed by hill or shore,
  They gave the song a voice,
Till all the craggy land had heard
  The Father's Faith rejoice.

3 And still it moves, a broadening flood;
  And fresher, fuller grows,
A sense as if the sea were near,
  Towards which the river flows!
O Thou, who art the secret Source
  That rises in each soul,
Thou art the Ocean too,—Thy charm,
  That ever deepening roll!

## 14                       6. 6. 4.

1 All hail, God's angel, Truth!
In whose immortal youth
  Fresh graces shine:
To her sweet majesty,
LORD, help us bend the knee,
And all her beauty see,
  And wealth divine.

2 Thanks for the names that light
The path of Truth and Right
  And Freedom's way:
For all whose life doth prove
The might of Faith, Hope, Love,
Thousands of hearts to move,
  A power to-day!

3 Thanks for the heart of Love,
   Kin to Thine own above,
       Tender and brave ;
   Ready to bear the cross,
   To suffer pain and loss,
   And earthly good count dross,
       In toils to save.

4 May their dear memory be
   True guide, O LORD, to Thee,
       With saints of yore ;
   And may the work they wrought,
   The truth of God they taught,
   The good for man they sought,
       Spread evermore !

## 15                                                          10s.

1 Eternal Ruler of the ceaseless round
    Of circling planets singing on their way,
  Guide of the nations from the night profound
    Into the glory of the perfect day,
  Rule in our hearts that we may ever be
  Guided and strengthened and upheld by
       Thee.

2 We are of Thee, the children of Thy love,
    The brothers of Thy well-belovèd Son ;
  Descend, O Holy Spirit, like a dove,

Into our hearts that we may be as one—
As one with Thee, to whom we ever tend;
As one with Him, our Brother and our Friend.

3 We would be one in hatred of all wrong,
One in our love of all things sweet and fair,
One with the joy that breaketh into song,
One with the grief that trembles into prayer,
One in the power that makes Thy children free
To follow truth, and thus to follow Thee.

4 O clothe us with Thy heavenly armor, Lord,—
Thy trusty shield, Thy sword of love divine.
Our inspiration be Thy constant word;
We ask no victories that are not Thine.
Give or withhold, let pain or pleasure be,
Enough to know that we are serving Thee.

## 16        6s

1 Upon one land alone
Has shone the holy light,
And all the world beside
Been left to walk in night?

2 Are only Christian men
  The children of the Lord,
And have none others heard
  The true life-giving word?

3. Is there one only name
    In all the tribes of earth,
  Through which the longing soul
    May find its higher birth?

4. Nay, every land is Thine;
    All men Thy children be;
  And every name of truth
    A star that leads to Thee.

## 17          8s.

1 Out from the heart of nature rolled
  The burdens of the Bible old;
  The litanies of nations came,
  Like the volcano's tongue of flame,
  Up from the burning core below,
  The canticles of love and woe.

2 The word unto the prophet spoken
  Was writ on tables yet unbroken,—
  Still floats upon the morning wind,
  Still whispers to the willing mind.
  One accent of the Holy Ghost
  The heedless world has never lost.

18                                     7s.

1 Life of Ages, richly poured,
    Soul of Worlds, unspent and free,
Nature's uncreated Word,
    Atom and Infinity!

2 Secret of the morning stars,
    Motion of the oldest hours,
Pledge through elemental wars
    Of the coming spirit's powers!

3 Rolling planet, flaming sun,
    Stand in nobler man complete;
Prescient laws Thine errands run,
    Frame a shrine for Godhead meet.

4 Homeward led, his wondering eye
    Upward yearned, in joy or awe,
Found the love that waited nigh,
    Guidance of Thy guardian Law.

5 In the touch of earth it thrilled;
    Down from mystic skies it burned;
Right obeyed and passion stilled,
    Its eternal gladness earned.

6 Still the immortal flame upspeeds,
    Kindling worlds to pure desire;
Where the unerring Spirit leads,
    Ages wonder and aspire.

19                                                          7s.

1 Life of Ages, richly poured,
    Love of God, unspent and free,
  Flowing in the prophet's word
    And the people's liberty !

2 Never was to chosen race
    That unstinted tide confined ;
  Thine is every time and place,
    Fountain sweet of heart and mind !

3 Breathing in the thinker's creed,
    Pulsing in the hero's blood,
  Nerving simplest thought and deed,
    Freshening time with truth and good ;

4 Consecrating art and song,
    Holy book and pilgrim track,
  Hurling floods of tyrant wrong
    From the sacred limits back,—

5 Life of Ages, richly poured,
    Love of God, unspent and free,
  Flow still in the prophet's word
    And the people's liberty !

## B. Hymns of Natural, Ethical and Spiritual Religion

## B. Hymns of Natural, Ethical and Spiritual Religion

**20**  10. 10. 11. 11.

1 O worship the King, all-glorious above!
 O gratefully sing His power and His love!
 Our Shield and Defender, the Ancient of Days,
 Pavilioned in splendor, and girded with praise.

2 The earth with its store of wonders untold,
 Almighty, Thy power hath founded of old;
 Hath stablished it fast by a changeless decree,
 And round it hath cast, like a mantle, the sea.

3 Thy bountiful care what tongue can recite?
 It breathes in the air, it shines in the light;

It streams from the hills, it descends to the plain,
And sweetly distils in the dew and the rain.

4 Frail children of dust, and feeble as frail,
In Thee do we trust, nor find Thee to fail;
Thy mercies how tender, how firm to the end,
Our Maker, Defender, Redeemer, and Friend!

5 O measureless Might, ineffable Love,
While angels delight to hymn Thee above,
Thy ransomed creation, though feeble their lays,
With true adoration shall sing to Thy praise.

**21**  11s.

1 Immortal, invisible, God only wise,
In light inaccessible hid from our eyes,
Most blessed, most glorious, the Ancient of Days,
Almighty, victorious, Thy great name we praise.

2 Unresting, unhasting, and silent as light,
Nor wanting, nor wasting, Thou rulest in might;

Thy justice like mountains high soaring above
Thy clouds, which are fountains of goodness and love.

3 To all, life Thou givest—to both great and small ;
In all life Thou livest, the true life of all ;
We blossom and flourish as leaves on the tree,
And wither and perish—but nought changeth Thee.

4 To-day and To-morrow with Thee still are Now ;
Nor trouble, nor sorrow, nor care, LORD, hast Thou ;
Nor passion doth fever, nor age doth decay,
The same God forever that was yesterday.

5 Great Father of glory, pure Father of light,
Thine angels adore Thee, all veiling their sight ;
But of all Thy rich graces this grace, LORD, impart,—
Take the veil from our faces, the veil from our heart.

**22**  7. 6.

1 O Father of our spirits,
  Whence life, love, beauty roll
Unasked, full, like a river
  To every human soul,
We thank Thee for our coming
  Into this world of Thine,
Voice of eternal silence,
  Stream from the sea divine.

2 For the green earth we thank Thee,
  With beast, and bird, and tree;
For sky that o'er us floateth,
  So blue, so bright, so free;
Thanks for the morning sunshine,
  And for the living air;
For sight of man, earth, heaven,
  Thy universe so fair;

3 Thanks for the world's great gospel,
  That dawned on eastern shore,
God loves the bird, the flower,
  He loveth man much more;
For no neglects or follies
  Will God a man e'er shun,
Forever and forever
  He loves and seeks His son.

4 And man for man his brother
  Throughout the world shall care,

And plenty, freedom, wisdom,
   Each shall with other share.
Who in man's form appeareth
   Beneath the outspread sky,
Shall call forth awe and service,
   As home of Deity.

5 Thanks for the holy circle
   In deathless friendship bound,
Who with us work and worship,
   Or sleep beneath the ground :
Oh, that our lives so gifted,
   Our daily thoughts and ways,
May make to ear of Heaven,
   Unbroken hymns of praise !

**23**                      L. M.

1 God of the earth, the sky, the sea !
   Maker of all above, below !
Creation lives and moves in Thee,
   Thy present life through all doth flow.

2 Thee in the lonely woods we meet,
   On the bare hills or cultured plains,
In every flower beneath our feet,
   And e'en the still rock's mossy stains.

3 Thy love is in the sunshine's glow,
   Thy life is in the quickening air ;

> When lightnings flash and storm-winds blow,
> There is Thy power, Thy law is there.

4 We feel Thy calm at evening's hour,
> Thy grandeur in the march of night;
> And, when the morning breaks in power,
> We hear Thy word, "Let there be light!"

5 But higher far, and far more clear,
> Thee in man's spirit we behold;
> Thine image and Thyself are there,—
> Th' Indwelling God, proclaimed of old.

**24**            11. 10.

1 I cannot find Thee. Still on restless pinion
> My spirit beats the void where Thou dost dwell;
> I wander lost through all Thy vast dominion,
> And shrink beneath Thy light ineffable.

2 I cannot find Thee. E'en when most adoring,
> Before Thy shrine I bend in lowliest prayer;

>   Beyond these bounds of thought, my thought upsoaring,
>     From farthest quest comes back : Thou art not there.

3 Yet high above the limits of my seeing,
    And folded far within the inmost heart,
  And deep below the deeps of conscious being,
    Thy splendor shineth : there, O God ! Thou art.

4 I cannot lose Thee.  Still in Thee abiding,
    The end is clear, how wide soe'er I roam ;
  The law that holds the worlds my steps is guiding :
    And I must rest at last in Thee, my home.

**25**  C. M.

1 Go not, my soul, in search of Him,
    Thou wilt not find Him there,—
  Or in the depths of shadow dim,
    Or heights of upper air.

2 For not in far-off realms of space
    The Spirit hath its throne ;
  In every heart it findeth place
    And waiteth to be known.

3 Thought answereth alone to thought,
    And soul with soul hath kin ;
  The outward God he findeth not
    Who finds not God within.

4 And if the vision come to thee
    Revealed by inward sign,
  Earth will be full of Deity
    And with His glory shine !

5 Thou shalt not want for company
    Nor pitch thy tent alone ;
  The indwelling God will go with thee
    And show thee of His own.

6 O gift of gifts, O grace of grace,
    That God should condescend
  To make thy heart His dwelling-place
    And be thy daily Friend !

7 Then go not thou in search of Him,
    But to thyself repair ;
  Wait thou within the silence dim
    And thou shalt find Him there !

26                                                      7. 6.

1  He hides within the lily
    A strong and tender care,
  That wins the earth-born atoms
    To glory of the air;
  He weaves the shining garments
    Unceasingly and still,
  Along the quiet waters,
    In niches of the hill.

2  We linger at the vigil
    With Him who bent the knee
  To watch the old-time lilies
    In distant Galilee;
  And still the worship deepens
    And quickens into new,
  As, brightening down the ages,
    God's secret thrilleth through.

3  O Toiler of the lily,
    Thy touch is in the Man!
  No leaf that dawns to petal
    But hints the angel-plan.
  The flower-horizons open!
    The blossom vaster shows!
  We hear Thy wide worlds echo,—
    See how the lily grows!

4 Shy yearnings of the savage,
    Unfolding thought by thought,
  To holy lives are lifted,
    To visions fair are wrought;
  The races rise and cluster,
    And evils fade and fall,
  Till chaos blooms to beauty,
    Thy purpose crowning all!

**27**   C. M.

1 We pray no more, made lowly wise,
    For miracle and sign;
  Anoint our eyes to see within
    The common the divine.

2 "Lo here, lo there," no more we cry,
    Dividing with our call
  The mantle of Thy presence, LORD,
    That seamless covers all.

3 We turn from seeking Thee afar
    And in unwonted ways,
  To build from out our daily lives
    The temples of Thy praise.

4 And if Thy casual comings, LORD,
    To hearts of old were dear,
  What joy shall dwell within the faith
    That feels Thee ever near!

**Natural, Ethical and Spiritual Religion**

5 And nobler yet shall duty grow,
   And more shall worship be,
   When Thou art found in all our life
   And all our life in Thee.

## 28                     11. 10

1 Infinite Spirit, who art round us ever,
   In whom we float as motes in summer sky,
  May neither life nor death the sweet bond sever
   Which binds us to our unseen Friend on high :—

2 Unseen, yet not unfelt ; if any thought
   Has raised our minds from earth, a pure desire,
  A generous act, a noble purpose brought,
   It is Thy breath, O LORD, which fans the fire.

3 To me, the humblest of Thy creatures, kneeling,
   Conscious of weakness, ignorance, sin, and shame,
  Give such a force of holy thought and feeling
   That I may live to glorify Thy name ;—

4 That I may conquer base desire and pas-
     sion,
   That I may rise o'er selfish thought and
       will,
   O'ercome the world's allurement, threat,
       and fashion,
   Walk humbly, softly, leaning on Thee
       still.


**29**                                          C. M.

1 The Lord is in His Holy Place
     In all things near and far!
  Shekinah of the snowflake, He,
     And glory of the star,
  And secret of the April land
     That stirs the field to flowers,
  Whose little tabernacles rise
     To hold Him through the hours.


2 He hides himself within the love
     Of those whom we love best;
  The smiles and tones that make our homes
     Are shrines by Him possessed;
  He tents within the lonely heart
     And shepherds every thought;
  We find Him not by seeking long,—
     We lose Him not, unsought.

3 Our art may build its Holy Place,
   Our feet on Sinai stand,
But holiest of Holies knows
   No tread, no touch of hand;
The listening soul makes Sinai still
   Wherever we may be,
And in the vow, "Thy will be done!"
   Lies all Gethsemane.

## 30                       S. M.

1 Where is thy God, my soul?
   Is He within thy heart;
Or ruler of a distant realm
   In which thou hast no part?

2 Where is thy God, my soul?
   Only in stars and sun;
Or have the holy words of truth
   His light in every one?

3 Where is thy God, my soul?
   Confined to Scripture's page;
Or does His Spirit check and guide
   Thy spirit of each age?

4 O Ruler of the sky,
   Rule Thou within my heart;
O great Adorner of the world,
   Thy light of life impart.

5 Giver of holy words,
    Bestow Thy holy power,
And aid me, whether work or thought
    Engage the varying hour.

6 In Thee have I my help,
    As all my fathers had;
I'll trust Thee when I'm sorrowful,
    And serve Thee when I'm glad.

**31**                                                                                           P. M.

1 The King of love my Shepherd is,
    Whose goodness faileth never;
I nothing lack if I am His,
    And He is mine forever.

2 Where streams of living water flow
    My ransomed soul He leadeth,
And, where the verdant pastures grow,
    With food celestial feedeth.

3 Perverse and foolish oft I strayed,
    But yet in love He sought me,
And on His shoulder gently laid,
    And home, rejoicing, brought me.

4 In death's dark vale I fear no ill
    With Thee, dear LORD, beside me;
Thy rod and staff my comfort still,
    Thy cross before to guide me.

5 Thou spread'st a table in my sight ;
    Thy unction grace bestoweth ;
And oh, what transport of delight
    From Thy pure chalice floweth !

6 And so through all the length of days
    Thy goodness faileth never :
Good Shepherd, may I sing Thy praise
    Within Thy house forever.

## 32                6s.

1 O Love that casts out fear,
    O Love that casts out sin,
Tarry no more without,
    But come and dwell within !

2 True sunlight of the soul,
    Surround us as we go ;
So shall our way be safe,
    Our feet no straying know.

3 Great love of God, come in !
    Well-spring of heavenly peace ;
Thou Living Water, come !
    Spring up, and never cease.

## 33             7. 7. 7. 5.

1 Mighty Spirit, gracious Guide,
    Let Thy light in us abide ;

>   Ever walking by Thy side,
>     Grant us heavenly love!

2 Love is kind, and suffers long;
  Love is meek, and thinks no wrong;
  Love than death itself more strong:
    Therefore give us love.

3 Prophecy will fade away,
  Melting in the light of day;
  Love will ever with us stay:
    Therefore give us love.

4 Faith will vanish into sight;
  Hope be emptied in delight;
  Love in heaven will shine more bright:
    Therefore give us love.

5 Faith and hope and love we see
  Joining hand in hand agree;
  But the greatest of the three,
    And the best, is love.

6 From the overshadowing
  Of Thy gold and silver wing,
  Shed on us, who to Thee sing,
    Holy, heavenly love!

## 34
L.M.

1 O Love divine, that stoop'st to share
   Our sharpest pang, our bitterest tear!
   On Thee we cast each earth-born care;
   We smile at pain while Thou art near.

2 Though long the weary way we tread,
   And sorrows crown each lingering year,
   No path we shun, no darkness dread,
   Our hearts still whispering, "Thou art near."

3 When drooping pleasure turns to grief,
   And trembling faith is changed to fear,
   The murmuring wind, the quivering leaf,
   Shall softly tell us Thou art near.

4 On Thee we cast our burdening woe,
   O Love divine, forever dear!
   Content to suffer while we know,
   Living or dying, Thou art near.

## 35
8s.

1 Thou hidden love of God, whose height,
   Whose depth unfathomed, no man knows,
   I see from far thy beauteous light,
   Inly I sigh for thy repose;
   My heart is pained, nor can it be
   At rest, till it finds rest in Thee.

2 Is there a thing beneath the sun
    That strives with Thee my heart to share?
Ah, tear it thence, and reign alone,
    The Lord of every motion there!
Then shall my heart from earth be free,
When it hath found repose in Thee!

3 O Love, thy sovereign aid impart,
    To save me from low-thoughted care;
Chase this self-will through all my heart,
    Through all its hidden mazes there;
Make me the loving child, that I
Ceaseless may Abba, Father, cry!

4 Each moment draw from earth away
    My heart, that lowly waits Thy call;
Speak to my inmost soul, and say,
    I am thy love, thy God, thy all!
To feel Thy power, to hear Thy voice,
To know Thy truth, be all my choice.

## 36      8s.

1 Let all men know, that all men move
Under a canopy of love,
As broad as the blue sky above;
That doubt and trouble, fear and pain,
And anguish, all are shadows vain;
That death itself shall not remain.

2 That weary deserts we may tread,
  A dreary labyrinth we may thread,
  Through dark ways underground be led;
  Yet, if we will our Guide obey,
  The dreariest path, the darkest way,
  Still issue out in heavenly day!

3 And we on divers shores now cast,
  Shall meet, our perilous voyage past,
  All in our Father's house at last!
  Let all men count it true that love,
  Blessing, not cursing, rules above,
  And that in it we live and move.

## 37     S. M.

1 At first I prayed for Light:—
    Could I but see the way,
  How gladly, swiftly would I walk
    To everlasting day!

2 And next I prayed for Strength:—
    That I might tread the road
  With firm, unfaltering feet, and win
    The heavens' serene abode.

3 And then I asked for Faith:—
    Could I but trust my God,
  I'd live enfolded in His peace,
    Though foes were all abroad.

4 But now I pray for Love :
    Deep love to God and man ;
    A living love that will not fail ;
    However dark his plan ;—

5 And Light and Strength and Faith
    Are opening everywhere !
    God only waited for me till
    I prayed the larger prayer.

## 38                          8. 8. 8. 2. 7.

1 LORD of might and LORD of glory,
Humbly do I bow before Thee,
With my whole heart I adore Thee,
    Great LORD !
Listen to my cry, O LORD.

2 Passions proud and fierce have ruled me,
Fancies light and vain have fooled me,
But Thy training stern has schooled me ;
    Now, LORD,
Take me for Thy child, O LORD !

3 Groping dim and bending lowly
Mortal vision catcheth slowly
Glimpses of the pure and holy ;
    Now, LORD,
Open Thou mine eyes, O LORD !

4 In the deed that no man knoweth,
  Where no praiseful trumpeth bloweth,
  Where he may not reap who soweth,
      There, LORD,
  Let my heart serve Thee, O, LORD.

## 39                       6. 7.

1 Now thank we all our God,
    With hearts and hands and voices,
  Who wondrous things hath done,
    In whom this world rejoices;
  Who from our mother's arms
    Hath blessed us on our way
  With countless gifts of love,
    And still is ours to-day.

2 Oh, may this beauteous God
    Through all our life be near us,
  With ever joyful hearts
    And blessed peace to cheer us,
  And keep us in His grace,
    And guide us when perplexed,
  And keep us safe from ill,
    In this life and the next.

## 40                 6. 5. Double.

1 Early will I seek Thee,
    God, my refuge strong;
  Late prepare to meet Thee

With my evening song.
Though unto Thy greatness
I with trembling soar,
Yet my inmost thinking
Lies Thine eyes before.

2 What this frail heart dreameth,
And my tongue's poor speech—
Can that even distant
To Thy greatness reach?
Being great in mercy,
Thou wilt not despise
Praises which till death's hour
From my soul shall rise.

**41**                              7. 6.

1 Brief life is here our portion,
   Brief sorrow, short-lived care;
The life that knows no ending,
   The tearless life is there!
O happy retribution!
   Short toil, eternal rest,
For mortals and for sinners,
   A mansion with the blest!

2 And now we fight the battle,
   But then shall wear the crown
Of full and everlasting
   And passionless renown;

  And He whom now we trust in
   Shall then be seen and known,
  And they that know and see Him
   Shall have Him for their own.

3 The morning shall awaken,
  The shadows flee away,
And each true-hearted servant
  Shall shine as doth the day ;
For God, our King and Portion,
  In fulness of His grace,
We then shall see forever,
  And worship face to face.

## 42              L. M.

1 Thou One in all, Thou All in one,
  Source of the grace that crowns our days,
For all Thy gifts 'neath cloud or sun
  We lift to Thee our grateful praise.

2 We bless Thee for the life that flows,
  A pulse in every grain of sand,
A beauty in the blushing rose,
  A thought and deed in brain and hand.

3 For life that Thou hast made a joy,
  For strength to make our lives like Thine,

For duties that our hands employ,—
　　We bring our offerings to Thy shrine.

4 Be Thine to give and ours to own
　　The truth that sets Thy children free,
　The law that binds us to Thy throne,
　　The love that makes us one with Thee.

## 43　　　　　　　　　　　　　　　　C. M.

1 Thou long disowned, reviled, oppressed,
　　Strange friend of human kind,
　Seeking through weary years a rest
　　Within our hearts to find ;—

2 How late thy bright and awful brow
　　Breaks through these clouds of sin :
　Hail, Truth divine, we know thee now,
　　Angel of God, come in.

3 Come, though with purifying fire,
　　And swift-dividing sword,
　Thou of all nations the desire ;
　　Earth waits thy cleansing word.

4 Struck by the lightning of thy glance,
　　Let old oppressions die ;
　Before thy cloudless countenance
　　Let fear and falsehood fly.

5 Anoint our eyes with healing grace,
    To see, as not before,
  Our Father in our brother's face,
    Our Maker in His poor.

6 Flood our dark life with golden day;
    Convince, subdue, enthrall;
  Then to a mightier yield thy sway,
    And Love be all in all.

## 44                            L. M.

1 O God, in whom we live and move,
Thy love is law, Thy law is love;
Thy present spirit waits to fill
The soul which comes to do Thy will.

2 Unto Thy children's spirits teach
Thy love, beyond the power of speech;
And make them know, with joyful awe,
The encircling presence of Thy law.

3 That law doth give to truth and right,
Howe'er despised, a conquering might,
And makes each fondly worshipped lie
And boasting wrong to cower and die.

4 Its patient working doth fulfil
Man's hope and God's all-perfect will,
Nor suffers one true word or thought
Or deed of love to come to nought.

5 Such faith, O God, our spirits fill,
That we may work in patience still;
Who works for justice works with Thee,
Who works in love, Thy child shall be.

## 45     C. M.

1 I worship Thee, sweet Will of God;
And all Thy ways adore;
And every day I live, I long
To love Thee more and more.

2 When obstacles and trials seem
Like prison-walls to be,
I do the little I can do,
And leave the rest to Thee.

3 I have no cares, O blessèd Will,
For all my cares are Thine;
I live in triumph, LORD, for Thou
Hast made Thy triumphs mine.

4 Man's weakness waiting upon God
Its end can never miss;
For men on earth no work can do
More angel-like than this.

5 Ride on, ride on triumphantly,
Thou glorious Will, ride on;
Faith's pilgrim sons behind Thee take
The road that Thou hast gone.

6 He always wins who sides with God,
    To him no chance is lost:
God's will is sweetest to him when
    It triumphs at his cost.

7 Ill that God blesses is our good,
    And unblest good is ill;
And all is right that seems most wrong,
    If it be His dear will.

## 46      C. M.

1 Eternal Life, whose love divine
    Enfolds us each and all,
We know no other truth than Thine,
    We heed no other call.

2 O may we serve in thought and deed
    Thy kingdom yet to be,
Till Truth and Righteousness and Love
    Shall lead all souls to Thee.

## 47      11. 10.

1 Father, to Thee we look in all our sorrow,
    Thou art the fountain whence our healing flows,
Dark though the night, joy cometh with the morrow;
    Safely they rest who in Thy love repose

2 Nought shall affright us on Thy goodness
        leaning,
    Low in the heart faith singeth still her
        song;
  Chastened by pains we learn life's deeper
        meaning,
    And in our weakness Thou dost make us
        strong.

3 Patient, O heart, though heavy be thy sor-
        rows!
    Be not cast down, disquieted in vain;
  Yet shalt thou praise Him when these
        darkened furrows,
    Where now He plougheth, wave with
        golden grain.

## 48          6. 10.

1    Wilt Thou not visit me?
  The plant beside me feels Thy gentle dew;
    Each blade of grass I see
  From Thy deep earth its quickening moist-
        ure drew.

2    Wilt Thou not visit me?
  The morning calls on me with cheering
        tone,
    And every hill and tree
  Has but one voice, the voice of Thee
        alone.

3   Come! for I need Thy love
   More than the flower the dew, or grass the rain:
   Come, like Thy holy Dove,
   And, swift-descending, bid me live again.

4   Yes! Thou wilt visit me;
   Nor plant nor tree Thine eye delights so well,
   As when, from sin set free,
   Man's spirit comes with Thine in peace to dwell.

**49**                                                8. 8. 7.

1 Gracious Power, the world pervading,
   Blessing all, and none upbraiding,
      We are met to worship Thee;

2 Not in formal adorations,
   Nor with servile deprecations,
      But in spirit true and free.

3 By Thy wisdom mind is lighted,
   By Thy love the heart excited,
      Light and love all flow from Thee;

4 And the soul of thought and feeling,
   In the voice Thy praises pealing,
      Must Thy noblest homage be.

5 Not alone in our devotion,
　In all being, life, and motion,
　We the present Godhead see.

## 50                  7. 6. 7. 6. 7. 7.

1 Write Thy law upon my heart,
　　Inwardly abiding;
　Make it of my life a part,
　　Still my footsteps guiding.
　Till I in Thy courts appear,
　And to fall, no longer fear.

2 Pour Thy life into my soul
　　Which, with strong awaking,
　Urges onward to the goal
　　Till that day is breaking,
　When to will, to do, to see,
　One unbroken bliss shall be.

## 51                  L. M.

1 One Lord there is, all lords above,—
　His name is Truth, His name is Love,
　His name is Beauty, it is Light,
　His will is Everlasting Right.

2 But ah! to wrong what is His name?
　This Lord is a Consuming Flame
　To every wrong beneath the sun;
　He is One Lord, the Holy One.

3 Lord of the Everlasting Name,
  Truth, Beauty, Light, Consuming Flame!
  Shall I not lift my heart to Thee,
  And ask Thee, Lord, to rule in me?

4 If I be ruled in other wise
  My lot is cast with all that dies,
  With things that harm, and things that hate,
  And roam by night, and miss the Gate,—

5 Thy happy Gate, which leads us where
  Love is like sunshine in the air,
  And Love and Law are both the same,
  Named with the Everlasting Name.

## 52                       C. M.

1 My God, how wonderful Thou art,
    Thy majesty how bright,
  How beautiful Thy mercy-seat,
    In depths of burning light!

2 How dread are Thine eternal years,
    O everlasting Lord,
  By prostrate spirits day and night
    Incessantly adored!

3 How wonderful, how beautiful,
    The sight of Thee must be,
  Thine endless wisdom, boundless power,
    And awful purity!

4 Oh, how I fear Thee, living God,
    With deepest, tenderest fears,
  And worship Thee with trembling hope,
    And penitential tears!

5 Yet I may love Thee too, O LORD,
    Almighty as Thou art,
  For Thou hast stooped to ask of me
    The love of my poor heart.

## 53 S. M.

1 Breathe on me, Breath of God,
    Fill me with life anew,
  That I may love what Thou dost love,
    And do what Thou wouldst do!

2 Breathe on me, Breath of God,
    Until my heart is pure,
  Until with Thee I will one will,
    To do or to endure!

3 Breathe on me, Breath of God,
    Till I am wholly Thine,
  Till all this earthly part of me
    Glows with Thy fire divine!

4 Breathe on me, Breath of God,
    So I shall never die,
  But live with Thee the perfect life
    Of Thine eternity!

**54**                               7s. Double.

1 Haste not! haste not! do not rest!
   Bind the motto to thy breast;
   Bear it with thee as a spell;
   Storm or sunshine, guard it well!
   ‖:Heed not flowers that round thee bloom,
   Bear it onward to the tomb. :‖

2 Haste not! let no thoughtless deed
   Mar for aye the spirit's speed;
   Ponder well and know the right,
   Onward then with all thy might!
   ‖ : Haste not, years can ne'er atone
   For one reckless action done. :‖

3 Rest not! life is sweeping by,
   Go and dare before you die;
   Something mighty and sublime
   Leave behind to conquer time!
   ‖ : Grand it is to live for aye
   When these forms have passed away. :‖

4 Haste not! rest not! calmly wait:
   Meekly bear the storms of fate!
   Duty be the polar guide,
   Do the right whate'er betide!
   ‖ :Haste not! rest not! conflicts past,
   God shall crown thy work at last. :‖

## 55         7s.

1 Come, Thou Holy Spirit, come;
And from Thy celestial home
  Shed a ray of light divine:
Come, Thou Father of the poor,
Come, Thou source of all our store,
  Come, within our bosoms shine;

2 Thou of Comforters the best,
Thou the soul's most welcome guest,
  Sweet refreshment here below;
In our labor rest most sweet,
Grateful coolness in the heat,
  Solace in the midst of woe.

3 O most blessèd Light divine,
Shine within these hearts of Thine,
  And our inmost being fill:
Where Thou art not, man hath nought,
Nothing good in deed or thought,
  Nothing free from taint of ill.

4 Heal our wounds; our strength renew;
On our dryness pour Thy dew;
  Wash the stains of guilt away:
Bend the stubborn heart and will;
Melt the frozen, warm the chill;
  Guide the steps that go astray.

    5 On the faithful, who adore
       And confess Thee evermore,
          In Thy gracious gifts descend :
      Give them virtue's sure reward,
      Give them Thy salvation, LORD,
        Give them joys that never end.

## 56                                                 C. M.

1 O God of Truth, whose living Word
    Upholds whate'er hath breath,
Look down on Thy creation, LORD,
    Enslaved by sin and death.

2 Set up Thy standard, LORD, that we
    Who claim a heavenly birth
May march with Thee to smite the lies
    That vex Thy groaning earth.

3 We fight for truth, we fight for God,
    Poor slaves of lies and sin !
He who would fight for Thee on earth
    Must first be true within.

4 Then, God of Truth, for whom we long,
    Thou who wilt hear our prayer,
Do Thine own battle in our hearts,
    And slay the falsehood there.

5 Still smite! still burn! till nought is left
    But God's own truth and love;
Then, LORD, as morning dew come down,
    Rest on us from above.

6 Yea, come! then, tried as in the fire,
    From every lie set free,
Thy perfect truth shall dwell in us,
    And we shall live in Thee.

## 57         C. M.

1 O God! Whose thoughts are brightest light,
    Whose love runs always clear,
To whose kind wisdom sinning souls
    Amidst their sins are dear!

2 Sweeten my bitter-thoughted heart
    With charity like Thine,
Till self shall be the only spot
    On earth which does not shine.

3 Hard-heartedness dwells not with souls
    Round whom Thine arms are drawn;
And dark thoughts fade away in grace,
    Like cloud-spots in the dawn.

4 When we ourselves least kindly are,
    We deem the world unkind;

Dark hearts, in flowers where honey lies,
    Only the poison find.

5 But they have caught the way of God,
    To whom self lies displayed
In such clear vision as to cast
    O'er others' faults a shade.

6 All bitterness is from ourselves,
    All sweetness is from Thee;
Dear God! forevermore be Thou
    Fountain and fire in me!

## 58       S. M.

1 Give to the winds thy fears;
    Hope, and be undismayed;
God hears thy sighs and counts thy tears;
    God shall lift up thy head.

2 Through waves, through clouds and storms,
    He gently clears thy way:
Wait thou His time; so shall the night
    Soon end in joyous day.

3 He everywhere hath sway,
    And all things serve His might;
His every act pure blessing is,
    His path unsullied light.

4 Leave to His sovereign sway
   To choose and to command:
With wonder filled, thou then shalt own
   How wise, how strong His hand.

5 Thou comprehend'st Him not:
   Yet earth and heaven tell
God sits as sovereign on the throne;
   He ruleth all things well.

## 59
C. M.

1 Firm, in the maddening maze of things,
   And tossed by storm and flood,
To one fixed state my spirit clings,—
   I know that God is good.

2 Not mine to look where cherubim
   And seraphs may not see,—
But nothing can be good in Him
   Which evil is in me.

3 The wrong that pains my soul below
   I dare not throne above;
I know not of His hate—I know
   His goodness and His love.

4 And Thou, O LORD, by whom are seen
   Thy creatures as they be,
Forgive me if too close I lean
   My human heart on Thee!

## 60          D. L. M.

1. To Thee we give ourselves to-day,
    Forgetful of the world outside,
We tarry in Thy house, O God,
    From eventide to eventide.
From Thine all-searching righteous eye
    Our deepest heart can nothing hide;
It crieth out for Thee, for peace,
    From eventide to eventide.

2. Who could endure shouldst Thou, O God,
    As we deserve, forever chide?
We therefore seek Thy pardoning grace
From eventide to eventide.
    Oh, may we lay to heart how swift
The years of life do onward glide;
    And learn to live that we may see
Thy light at our own eventide.

## 61          S. M.

1. God of the earnest heart,—
    The trust assured and still,
Thou who our strength forever art,
    We come to do Thy will!

2. Upon that painful road
    By saints serenely trod,
Whereon their hallowing influence flowed,
    Would we go forth, O God;

3 'Gainst doubt and shame and fear
   In human hearts to strive,
That all may learn to love and bear,
   To conquer self, and live;

4 To draw Thy blessing down,
   And bring the wronged redress,
And give this glorious world its crown,
   The Spirit's Godlikeness.

5 No dreams from toil to charm,
   No trembling on the tongue,—
Lord, in Thy rest may we be calm,
   Through Thy completeness strong.

6 Thou hearest while we pray;
   Oh deep within us write,
With kindling power, our God, to-day,
   Thy word,—"On earth be light."

## 62
L. M.

1 Oh, sometimes gleams upon our sight,
Through present wrong, the Eternal Right,
And step by step, since time began,
We see the steady gain of man;

2 That all of good the past hath had
Remains to make our own time glad,
Our common, daily life divine,
And every land a Palestine.

3 We lack but open eye and ear,
   To find the Orient's marvels here;
   The still small voice in autumn's hush,
   Yon maple wood the burning bush.

4 For still the new transcends the old,
   In signs and tokens manifold;
   Slaves rise up men; the olive waves,
   With roots deep set in battle graves.

5 Through the harsh noises of our day
   A low, sweet prelude finds its way;
   Through clouds of doubt, and creeds of fear,
   A light is breaking calm and clear.

6 Henceforth my heart shall sigh no more
   For olden time and holier shore:
   God's love and blessing, then and there,
   And now and here and everywhere.

## 63         6s.

1 We name Thy name, O God,
   As our God call on Thee,
  Though the dark heart meantime
   Far from Thy ways may be.

2 And we can own Thy law,
   And we can sing Thy songs,

    While this sad inner soul
        To sin and shame belongs.

3 On us Thy love may glow,
    As the pure midday fire
On some foul spot look down ;
    And yet the mire be mire.

4 Then spare us not Thy fires,
    The searching light and pain ;
Burn out the sin ; and, last,
    With Thy love heal again.

## 64                                 C. M.

1 Walk in the light ! so shalt thou know
    That fellowship of love
His Spirit only can bestow,
    Who reigns in light above.

2 Walk in the light ! and thou shalt find
    Thy heart made truly His,
Who dwells in cloudless light enshrined,
    In whom no darkness is.

3 Walk in the light ! and thou shalt own
    Thy darkness passed away ;
Because that light hath on thee shone
    In which is perfect day.

4 Walk in the light! and thine shall be
    A path, though thorny, bright;
For God, by grace, shall dwell in thee,
    And God Himself is Light.

### 65                                     S. M.

1 Give forth thine earnest cry,
    O conscience, voice of God!
To young and old, to low and high,
    Proclaim His will abroad.

2 Within the human breast
    The strong monitions plead,
Still thunder Thy divine protest
    Against th' unrighteous deed.

3 Show the true way of peace
    O Thou, our guiding light!
From bondage of the wrong release
    To service of the right.

### 66                                     S M.

1  O Everlasting Light!
    Giver of dawn and day,
Dispeller of the ancient night
    In which creation lay:

2 O everlasting Health!
    Flow through life's inmost springs;
  The heart's best bliss, the soul's best wealth,
    What life Thy presence brings!

3 O everlasting Truth!
    The soul of all that's true,
  Sure guide alike of age and youth,
    Lead me and teach me too.

4 O everlasting Might!
    My broken life repair;
  Nerve Thou my will, and clear my sight,
    Give strength to do and bear.

5 O everlasting Love!
    Wellspring of grace and peace;
  Pour down Thy fulness from above,
    Bid doubt and trouble cease!

## 67         10. 4.

1 Lead, kindly Light, amid the encircling gloom
    Lead Thou me on:
The night is dark, and I am far from home,
    Lead Thou me on.
Keep Thou my feet; I do not ask to see
The distant scene; one step enough for me.

2 I was not ever thus, nor prayed that Thou
        Shouldst lead me on ;
  I loved to choose and see my path ; but now
        Lead Thou me on.
I loved the garish day, and spite of fears,
Pride ruled my will : remember not past years.

3 So long Thy power hath blest me, sure it still
        Will lead me on,
O'er moor and fen, o'er crag and torrent, till
        The night is gone,
And with the morn those angel faces smile
Which I have loved long since, and lost awhile.

## 68
11. 10.

1 Father, in Thy mysterious presence kneeling,
  Fain would our souls feel all Thy kindling love ;
  For we are weak, and need some deep revealing
    Of Trust and Strength and Calmness from above.

2 Lord, we have wandered forth through
    doubt and sorrow,
  And Thou hast made each step an on-
    ward one;
  And we will ever trust each unknown mor-
    row,—
  Thou wilt sustain us till its work is done.

3 In the heart's depths a peace serene and
    holy
  Abides; and when pain seems to have
    its will,
  Or we despair, oh, may that peace rise
    slowly,
  Stronger than agony, and we be still!

4 Now, Father, now, in Thy dear presence
    kneeling,
  Our spirits yearn to feel thy kindling
    love;
  Now make us strong, we need Thy deep
    revealing
    Of Trust and Strength and Calmness
      from above.

## 69 L. M.

1 Lord of all being! throned afar,
  Thy glory flames from sun and star;

Centre and soul of every sphere,
Yet to each loving heart how near!

2 Sun of our life! Thy quickening ray
Sheds on our path the glow of day;
Star of our hope! Thy softened light
Cheers the long watches of the night.

3 Our midnight is Thy smile withdrawn;
Our noontide is Thy gracious dawn;
Our rainbow arch Thy mercy's sign:
All, save the clouds of sin, are Thine.

4 Lord of all life, below, above,
Whose light is Truth, whose warmth is Love;
Before Thy ever-blazing throne
We ask no lustre of our own.

5 Grant us Thy truth to make us free,
And kindling hearts that burn for Thee,
Till all Thy living altars claim
One holy light, one heavenly flame.

**70**                                                7s.

1 What Thou wilt, O Father, give!
All is gain that I receive;
Let the lowliest task be mine,
Grateful, so the work be Thine.

2 Let me find the humblest place
  In the shadow of Thy grace;
  Let me find in Thine employ
  Peace, that dearer is than joy.

3 If there be some weaker one,
  Give me strength to help him on;
  If a blinder soul there be,
  Let me guide him nearer Thee.

4 Make my mortal dreams come true
  With the work I fain would do;
  Clothe with life the weak intent,
  Let me be the thing I meant!

5 Out of self to love be led,
  And to heaven acclimated,
  Until all things sweet and good
  Seem my natural habitude.

**71**  8s.

1 Thou hidden source of calm repose,
    Thou all-sufficient Love divine,
  My help and refuge from my foes,
    Secure I am if Thou art mine.
  From sin, and grief, and shame I fly,
  To shelter in Thy fortress high.

2 In want my plentiful supply,
   In weakness my Almighty power,
In bonds my perfect liberty,
   My light in dark temptation's hour,
In grief my joy unspeakable,
My life in death, my heaven in hell.

3 Thee will I love, my strength, my tower!
   Thee will I love, my joy, my crown;
Thee will I love with all my power,
   In all Thy works and Thee alone!
And though my flesh and heart decay
Thee shall I love in endless day.

## 72                 C. P. M.

1 LORD God, by whom all change is wrought,
By whom new things to light are brought,
   In whom no change is known!
Whate'er Thou dost, whate'er Thou art,
Thy children still in Thee have part;
   Still, still, Thou art our own.

2 Spirit, who makest all things new!
   Thou leadest onward; we pursue
      The heavenly march sublime.
In Thy renewing fire we glow,
And still from strength to strength we go,
      From height to height we climb.

3 Darkness and dread we leave behind;
　New light, new glory still we find,
　　New realms divine possess;
　New births of good, new conquests bring,
　Until triumphant we shall sing
　　In perfect Holiness.

**73**　　　　　　　　　　　8. 7. Double

1 Courage, brother! do not stumble
　　Though thy path be dark as night;
　There's a star to guide the humble:
　　'Trust in God and do the right.'
　Though the road be long and dreary,
　　And its ending out of sight:
　Foot it bravely—strong or weary:
　　'Trust in God, and do the right.'

2 Trust no party, church, or faction,
　　Trust no leaders in the fight,
　But in every word and action
　　'Trust in God, and do the right.'
　Some will hate thee, some will love thee,
　　Some will flatter, some will slight;
　Cease from man, and look above thee:
　　'Trust in God, and do the right.'

3 Trust no forms of guilty passion,
　　Fiends can look like angels bright;

Trust no custom, school, or fashion,
   'Trust in God, and do the right.'
Simple rule and safest guiding,
   Inward peace and inward light.
Star upon our path abiding,
   'Trust in God, and do the right.'

## 74     L. M.

1 Thou LORD of Hosts, whose guiding hand
   Hast brought us here before Thy face;
Our spirits wait for Thy command,
   Our silent hearts implore Thy peace.

2 Our spirits lay their noblest powers,
   As offering, on Thy holy shrine:
Thine was the strength that nourished ours,—
   The soldiers of the Cross are Thine.

3 While watching on our arms at night,
   We saw Thine angels round us move;
We heard Thy call, we felt Thy light,
   And followed, trusting to Thy love.

4 And now with hymn and prayer we stand,
   To give our strength to Thee, great God:
We would redeem Thy holy land,
   That land which sin so long has trod.

5 Send us where'er Thou wilt, O LORD!
 Through rugged toil and wearying fight :
Thy conquering love shall be our sword,
 And faith in Thee our truest might.

6 Send down Thy constant aid, we pray ;
 Be Thy pure angels with us still :
Thy Truth, be that our firmest stay :
 Our only rest, to do Thy will.

## 75                C. M.

1 O God, our Help in ages past,
 Our Hope for years to come,
Our Shelter from the stormy blast,
 And our eternal Home :

2 Under the shadow of Thy Throne
 Thy saints have dwelt secure ;
Sufficient is Thine arm alone,
 And our defence is sure.

3 Before the hills in order stood,
 Or earth received her frame,
From everlasting Thou art God,
 To endless years the same.

4 A thousand ages in Thy sight
 Are like an evening gone ;

Short as the watch that ends the night
      Before the rising sun.

5 Time, like an ever-rolling stream,
      Bears all its sons away ;
   They fly forgotten, as a dream
      Dies at the opening day.

6 O God, our Help in ages past,
      Our Hope for years to come,
   Be Thou our Guide while life shall last
      And our eternal Home !

# C. Hymns of Religion—Society and the State

## C. Hymns of Religion—Society and the State

**76**  6s.

1 God of Might, God of Right,
   Thee we give all glory;
Thine all praise in these days
   As in ages hoary,
When we hear, year by year,
   Freedom's wondrous story.

2 Now as erst, when Thou first
   Mad'st the proclamation,
Warning loud every proud,
   Every tyrant nation,
We Thy fame still proclaim,
   Bend in adoration.

3 Be with all, who in thrall
   To their task are driven;
In Thy power speed the hour
   When our chains are riven;

Earth around will resound
Gleeful hymns to heaven.

## 77         7s.

1 Men, whose boast it is, that ye
Come of fathers, brave and free,
If there breathe on earth a slave,
Are ye truly free and brave?
If ye do not feel the chain
When it works a brother's pain,
Are ye not base slaves, indeed,
Slaves unworthy to be freed?

2 Is true freedom but to break
Fetters for our own dear sake,
And with heathen hearts forget
That we owe mankind a debt?
No, true freedom is to share
All the chains our brothers wear,
And with heart and hand to be
Earnest to make others free.

3 They are slaves who fear to speak
For the fallen and the meek;
They are slaves who will not choose
Hatred, scoffing, and abuse
Rather than in silence shrink

From the truth they needs must think;
They are slaves who dare not be
In the right with two or three.

## 78     C. M.

1 Oh, it is hard to work for God,
    To rise and take His part
Upon this battle-field of earth,
    And not sometimes lose heart.

2 He hides Himself so wondrously,
    As though there were no God;
He is least seen when all the powers
    Of ill are most abroad.

3 Workman of God, oh, lose not heart,
    But learn what God is like;
And in the darkest battle-field
    Thou shalt know where to strike.

4 Thrice blest is he to whom is given
    The instinct that can tell
That God is on the field when He
    Is most invisible.

5 Blest too is he who can divine
    Where real right doth lie,
And dares to take the side that seems
    Wrong to man's blindfold eye.

6 Muse on His justice, downcast soul,
    Muse, and take better heart;
Back with thine angel to the field,
    And bravely do thy part.

7 For right is right, since God is God;
    And right the day must win;
To doubt would be disloyalty,
    To falter would be sin.

## 79     11. 10.

1 He whom the Master loved has truly spoken:—
    The holier worship, which God deigns to bless,
Restores the lost, binds up the spirit-broken,
    And feeds the widow and the fatherless.

2 O brother man! fold to thy heart thy brother;
    For where love dwells the peace of God is there;
To worship rightly is to love each other;
    Each smile a hymn, each kindly deed a prayer.

3 Follow with reverent steps the great example
   Of Him whose holy work was doing good:
 So shall the wide earth seem our Father's temple,
   Each loving life a psalm of gratitude.

4 Then shall all shackles fall; the stormy clangor
   Of wild war-music o'er the earth shall cease;
 Love shall tread out the baleful fire of anger,
   And in its ashes plant the tree of peace.

## 80                            7s.

1 Father, let Thy kingdom come,—
   Let it come with living power;
 Speak at length the final word,
   Usher in the triumph hour!

2 As it came in days of old,
   In the deepest hearts of men,
 When Thy martyrs died for Thee,
   Let it come, O God, again!

3 Tyrant thrones and idol shrines,
    Let them from their place be hurled:
Enter on Thy better reign,—
    Wear the crown of this poor world!

4 Oh, what long, sad years have gone
    Since Thy Church was taught this prayer!
Oh, what eyes have watched and wept
    For the dawning everywhere!

5 Break, triumphant day of God!
    Break at last, our hearts to cheer;
Throbbing souls and holy songs
    Wait to hail thy dawning here.

6 Empires, temples, sceptres, thrones,—
    May they all for God be won!
And, in every human heart,
    Father, let Thy kingdom come!

## 81                               L. M.

1 O God of love, O King of peace,
Make wars throughout the world to cease;
The wrath of sinful man restrain,
Give peace, O God, give peace again!

2 Remember, LORD, Thy works of old,
The wonders that our fathers told;

  Remember not our sin's dark stain,
  Give peace, O God, give peace again!

3 Whom shall we trust but Thee, O LORD?
 Where rest but on Thy faithful word?
 None ever called on Thee in vain,
 Give peace, O God, give peace again!

4 Where saints and angels dwell above,
 All hearts are knit in holy love;
 Oh, bind us in that heavenly chain!
 Give peace, O God, give peace again!

**82**                S. 7.

1 Once to every man and nation
  Comes the moment to decide,
 In the strife of Truth with Falsehood,
  For the good or evil side;
 Some great cause, God's new Messiah,
  Offers each the bloom or blight,
 And the choice goes by forever
  'Twixt that darkness and that light.

2 Then to side with Truth is noble,
  When we share her wretched crust,
 Ere her cause bring fame and profit,
  And 't is prosperous to be just;

Then it is the brave man chooses,
  While the coward stands aside,
Till the multitude make virtue
  Of the faith they had denied.

3 Though the cause of Evil prosper,
  Yet 't is Truth alone is strong;
Though her portion be the scaffold,
  And upon the throne be Wrong,
Yet that scaffold sways the future,
  And, behind the dim unknown,
Standeth God within the Shadow,
  Keeping watch above His own.

**83**                 6. 6. 4.

1 God bless our native land!
Firm may she ever stand
  Through storm and night!
When the wild tempests rave,
Ruler of wind and wave,
Do Thou our country save,
  By Thy great might!

2 For her our prayers shall be,
Our fathers' God, to Thee,
  On Thee we wait!
Be her walls Holiness;
Her rulers, Righteousness;

  Her officers be Peace;
   God save the State!

3 Lord of all truth and right,
 In whom alone is might,
  On Thee we call!
 Give us prosperity;
 Give us true liberty;
 May all the oppressèd go free;
  God save us all!

## 84

1 O Beautiful, my Country,
 Be thine a nobler care
Than all thy wealth of commerce,
 Thy harvests waving fair:
Be it thy pride to lift up
 The manhood of the poor;
Be thou to the oppressèd
 Fair Freedom's open door!

2 For thee our fathers suffered,
 For thee they toiled and prayed;
Upon thy holy altar
 Their willing lives they laid.
Thou hast no common birthright,
 Grand memories on thee shine;
The blood of pilgrim nations
 Commingled flows in thine.

3 O Beautiful, our Country!
　　Round thee in love we draw:
　Thine is the grace of Freedom,
　　The majesty of Law.
　Be Righteousness thy sceptre,
　　Justice thy diadem;
　And on thy shining forehead
　　Be Peace the crowning gem!

**85**　　　　　　　6. 6. 4. 6. 6. 6. 4.

1 My country! 't is of thee,
　Sweet land of liberty,
　　Of thee I sing;
　Land where my fathers died!
　Land of the pilgrim's pride,
　From every mountain side,
　　Let freedom ring!

2 My native country! thee,—
　Land of the noble, free,—
　　Thy name I love;
　I love thy rocks and rills,
　Thy woods and templed hills;
　My heart with rapture thrills
　　Like that above.

3 Let music swell the breeze,
　And ring from all the trees,

Sweet Freedom's song:
Let mortal tongues awake;
Let all that breathe partake;
Let rocks their silence break,—
   The sound prolong.

4 Our fathers' God! to Thee,
Author of liberty,
   To Thee we sing:
Long may our land be bright,
With Freedom's holy light;
Protect us, by Thy might,
   Great God, our King!

# IV

# Index of Subjects and Sources

# Index of Subjects and Sources

## I. SCRIPTURE READINGS

### A. Jewish and Christian Sources

#### a. Universality in Religion

| SEC. | PAGE. | SUBJECT. | |
|---|---|---|---|
| 1 | 3 | Creation of man | Gen. i |
| 1 | 3 | Character of Joseph | Gen. xli |
| 1 | 3 | The Edomite a brother | Deut. xxiii |
| 1 | 4 | Cyrus the anointed | Isa. xlv |
| 1 | 4 | The Lord in His temple | Habak. ii |
| 1 | 4 | Great is the name of the Lord | Mal. i |
| 2 | 4 | Ben Zoma: Who is a wise man? | The Mishna |
| 2 | 5 | Ben Azzai: Virtue and vice | The Mishna |
| 2 | 5 | Rabbi Simeon: The three crowns | The Mishna |
| 2 | 6 | Rabbi Jacob: This world the antechamber to another | The Mishna |
| 2 | 6 | Rabbi Elazar Hakkapar: Accountability to God | The Mishna |
| 3 | 7 | The great commandment in the Law | Matt. xxii |

# Index of Subjects and Sources

| SEC. | PAGE. | SUBJECT. | |
|---|---|---|---|
| 3 | 7 | The kingdom of God | Luke xiii |
| 3 | 7 | God is a Spirit | John iv |
| 3 | 8 | "One flock, one shepherd" | John x |
| 4 | 8 | In the synagogue at Nazareth | Luke iv |
| 5 | 9 | The day of Pentecost | Acts ii |
| 6 | 10 | The true Light coming into the world | John i |
| 7 | 11 | Paul at Athens | Acts xvii |
| 8 | 12 | No respect of persons with God | Rom. ii, iii, viii, and x |
| 8 | 13 | Vocation of a Christian | Eph. v |

### b. ETHICAL AND SPIRITUAL RELIGION

| | | | |
|---|---|---|---|
| 9 | 17 | "Hear, O Israel" | Deut. vi |
| 9 | 17 | The commandment very nigh unto thee | Deut. xxx |
| 10 | 17 | "Shall mortal man be more just than God?" | Job iv |
| 11 | 18 | "Where shall wisdom be found?" | Job xxviii |
| 12 | 20 | The righteous man | Job xxix |
| 13 | 21 | Generosity and justice | Job xiii, xxiv, xxxi, and xxxvi |
| 14 | 23 | Who shall sojourn in the Lord's tabernacle? | Ps. xv |
| 15 | 24 | "The heavens declare the glory of God" | Ps. xix |
| 16 | 25 | "The Lord is my Shepherd" | Ps. xxiii |
| 17 | 26 | "The secret place of the Most High" | Ps. xci |
| 18 | 28 | "Bless the LORD, O my soul" | Ps. ciii |
| 19 | 30 | The man that findeth wisdom | Prov. viii |

# Index of Subjects and Sources

| SEC. | PAGE. | SUBJECT. | |
|---|---|---|---|
| 20 | 31 | The dwelling of wisdom | Prov. viii |
| 21 | 34 | The comfort of God's people | Isa. xl |
| 22 | 36 | A new covenant with the house of Israel | Jer. xxxi |
| 23 | 37 | The Lord's controversy with His people | Micah vi |
| 24 | 38 | The motto of Simon the Just | The Mishna |
| 24 | 38 | The rule of Antigonos of Sokho | The Mishna |
| 24 | 39 | Rabbi Joshua ben Pera'hya: Companionship | The Mishna |
| 24 | 39 | Rabbi Hillel: The disciple of Aaron | The Mishna |
| 24 | 39 | Rabban Simeon ben Gamaliel: The value of silence | The Mishna |
| 24 | 39 | Rabban Simeon ben Gamaliel: Three things support the world | The Mishna |
| 25 | 39 | Rabbi Judah: On choosing the right path | The Mishna |
| 25 | 40 | Rabbi Hillel: Spiritual interests immediate | The Mishna |
| 25 | 40 | Rabbi Hillel: Value of a good name | The Mishna |
| 25 | 41 | Rabbi Jo'hanan ben Zakkai: To his disciples | The Mishna |
| 25 | 41 | Rabbi José: Thy neighbor's property | The Mishna |
| 25 | 41 | Rabbi Simeon: The offering of prayer | The Mishna |
| 25 | 41 | Rabbi Tarphon: The day and the task | The Mishna |

| SEC. | PAGE. | SUBJECT. | |
|---|---|---|---|
| 26 | 42 | The Beatitudes | Matt. v |
| 27 | 43 | The providence of God | Matt. vii |
| 28 | 44 | Judgment and mercy | Matt. vii |
| 29 | 46 | Faith, hope, and charity abide | 1 Cor. xiii |
| 30 | 47 | The love of God and the love of the other | 1 John iii |

### C. RELIGION IN SOCIETY AND THE STATE

| | | | |
|---|---|---|---|
| 31 | 51 | The way of remembrance | Deut. vii |
| 32 | 53 | Release every seven years | Deut. xv |
| 32 | 54 | Obedience and welfare | Deut. xv |
| 33 | 55 | The year of jubile | Lev. xxv |
| 34 | 57 | The poor and the bondservant | Lev. xxv |
| 34 | 58 | The duty of the king | Ps. lxxii |
| 35 | 60 | The Lord's Anointed | Isa. xi |
| 36 | 61 | The true fast | Isa. lviii |
| 37 | 63 | Four views concerning property | The Mishna |
| 37 | 63 | Four classes of the charitable | The Mishna |
| 37 | 64 | Four classes among the disciples of the wise | The Mishna |
| 37 | 64 | Love without ulterior motive | The Mishna |
| 37 | 64 | Rabbi Judah ben Thema: Doing the will of God | The Mishna |
| 38 | 64 | Rabbi 'Haninah: Prayer for the government | The Mishna |
| 38 | 64 | Rabbi Eliezer of Bartotha: What is due God | The Mishna |
| 38 | 65 | Rabbi 'Haninah ben Dosa: Enduring wisdom | The Mishna |
| 38 | 65 | Rabbi Elazar ben Azariah: True culture | The Mishna |

## d. RESPONSIVE READINGS

| SEC. | PAGE. | SUBJECT. |
|---|---|---|
| 39–42 | 69–75 | From the Psalms |
| 43 | 75–78 | Sayings of Jesus |

## B. ETHNIC SCRIPTURES

[Hindu, Persian, Chinese, Egyptian, Buddhist, Grecian, Roman, and Mohammedan Sources.]

### a. UNIVERSALITY IN RELIGION

| | | | |
|---|---|---|---|
| 44 | 81 | Truth more than creed or prayer . . | From the Hindu (Schermerhorn's *Ancient Sacred Scriptures*) |
| 44 | 81 | The dwelling of God | From the Hindu (Schermerhorn) |
| 45 | 82 | The attainment of peace | From the Arabian (Schermerhorn) |
| 45 | 83 | Háfiz : The object of all religion . . | From the Persian (Conway's *Sacred Anthology*) |
| 45 | 83 | Divine Love the one doctrine | From the Persian (Conway) |
| 45 | 83 | The name of God | From the Persian (Conway) |
| 45 | 84 | The way to God | From the Persian (Conway) |
| 46 | 85 | Abraham and his guest | From the Persian (Conway) |
| 47 | 85 | Not posture but purpose required by religion | The Qur'án (Koran) |
| 48 | 87 | Men should not dispute about God . . . | From the Arabian (Schermerhorn) |

## b. ETHICAL AND SPIRITUAL RELIGION

| SEC. | PAGE. | SUBJECT. |
|---|---|---|
| 49 | 93 | God to whom sacrifice shall be offered . . Vedic Hymn (Sacred Books of the East, Edited by Prof. Max Müller) |
| 50 | 94 | "All this is Brahman" Khandogya-Upanishad (Müller) |
| 51 | 95 | The doctrine of the Self Khandogya-Upanishad. Vagasaneyi-Samhita Upanishad (Müller) |
| 52 | 96 | The mortal body the abode of the Self . Khandogya-Upanishad. Vagasaneyi-Samhita Upanishad (Müller) |
| 53 | 97 | The fruit of the Nayagrodha tree . Khandogya-Upanishad. Katha-Upanishad (Müller) |
| 54 | 98 | Where Brahman dwells Khandogya-Aitareya Aranyaka-Upanishad (Müller) |
| 55 | 100 | The highest Self Upanishads (Katha Khandogya, Mundaka, Taittiriyaka) (Müller) |
| 56 | 101 | The Dispenser of Life Upanishads (Müller) |
| 57 | 102 | The Supreme Unity Bhagavad-Gita (Müller) |
| 58 | 104 | The Deity within all forms Bhagavad-Gita (Müller) |
| 59 | 105 | Universal presence of God Hindu Hymn (Conway) |
| 60 | 105 | Happiness and Holiness Zend-Avesta (Müller) |

# Index of Subjects and Sources

| SEC. | PAGE. | SUBJECT. |
|---|---|---|
| 61 | 106 | Thoughts, words, and deeds |
| | | Zend-Avesta (Müller) |
| 62 | 108 | The Creator and Sustainer of the righteous |
| | | Zend-Avesta (Müller) |
| 63 | 109 | Parable of the fishes |
| | | From the Persian (Conway) |
| 64 | 110 | "The Attainment of the Aim" |
| | | Texts of Tâoism (Müller) |
| 65 | 112 | The conditions of life |
| | | Texts of Tâoism (Müller) |
| 66 | 114 | The constant mind |
| | | Texts of Tâoism (Müller) |
| 67 | 115 | The Heavenly Man |
| | | Texts of Tâoism (Müller) |
| 68 | 116 | Him to whom Heaven is all |
| | | Texts of Tâoism (Müller) |
| 69 | 117 | Deplorable conditions |
| | | Texts of Tâoism (Müller) |
| 70 | 119 | Reverence and harmony |
| | | Hsiaô King, Shu King, Shih King (Müller) |
| 71 | 120 | The superior man |
| | | The Li Ki (Müller) |
| 72 | 122 | Departing from iniquity |
| | | Egyptian Book of the Dead (Hibbert lectures 1879, Renouf) |
| 73 | 122 | The Ever Living |
| | | Egyptian Book of the Dead (Hibbert lectures 1879, Renouf) |
| 74 | 123 | The Eternity of God |
| | | Egyptian Book of the Dead (Hibbert lectures 1879, Renouf) |

# Index of Subjects and Sources

| SEC. | PAGE. | SUBJECT. |
|---|---|---|
| 75 | 125 | Amon-Rā, maker of all that is |
|  |  | Egyptian Book of the Dead (Hibbert lectures 1879, Renouf) |
| 76 | 127 | God immanent in all things |
|  |  | Egyptian Book of the Dead (Hibbert lectures 1879, Renouf) |
| 77 | 128 | To cease from sin |
|  |  | Dhammapada, Buddhist (Müller) |
| 78 | 131 | To overcome temptation |
|  |  | Dhammapada (Müller) |
| 79 | 132 | Good and evil thoughts and deeds . Dhammapada (Müller) |
| 80 | 134 | Do not follow the evil law |
|  |  | Dhammapada (Müller) |
| 81 | 135 | The way of the Awakened |
|  |  | Dhammapada (Müller) |
| 82 | 137 | Let a man leave anger |
|  |  | Dhammapada (Müller) |
| 83 | 137 | All created things perish |
|  |  | Dhammapada (Müller) |
| 84 | 138 | Who is a Brâhmana |
|  |  | Dhammapada (Müller) |
| 85 | 141 | They who dwell in the City of Righteousness |
|  |  | Milindapañha (Müller) |
| 86 | 144 | The effect testifies to its cause . Milindapañha (Müller) |
| 87 | 146 | The middle path . Buddhist (Müller) |
| 88 | 148 | Putting away evil things |
|  |  | On Conduct (Buddhist) |
| 89 | 150 | Prayer to Zeus |
|  |  | Hymn of Cleanthes (Greek) |

| SEC. | PAGE. | SUBJECT. |
|---|---|---|
| 90 | 152 | Socrates on the duty of a philosopher |
| | | Plato's Dialogues, The Apology (Jowett's Trans.) |
| 91 | 155 | Socrates on Life and Death |
| | | Plato's Dialogues, The Apology (Jowett's Trans.) |
| 92 | 158 | The Earth Dwellers |
| | | Plato's Dialogues, The Phædo (Jowett's Trans.) |
| 93 | 160 | Home of the Blessed |
| | | Plato's Dialogues, The Phædo (Jowett's Trans.) |
| 94 | 162 | The fair prize and great hope |
| | | Plato's Dialogues, The Phædo (Jowett's Trans.) |
| 95 | 164 | The divine beauty and order |
| | | Plato's Dialogues, Symposium (Jowett's Trans.) |
| 96 | 166 | True possessions |
| | | Plato: The Laws (Jowett's Trans.) |
| 97 | 167 | The regulation of life |
| | | Marcus Aurelius Antoninus: Meditations |
| 98 | 169 | What is due to one's self |
| | | Marcus Aurelius Antoninus |
| 99 | 171 | The universe one living Being |
| | | Marcus Aurelius Antoninus |
| 100 | 173 | Trust in him who governs |
| | | Marcus Aurelius Antoninus |

| SEC. | PAGE. | SUBJECT. | |
|---|---|---|---|
| 101 | 174 | My Country is the world | Marcus Aurelius Antoninus |
| 102 | 176 | The fountain of good is within | Marcus Aurelius Antoninus |
| 103 | 177 | To avoid ignoble and mean thoughts. | Epictetus Discourses |
| 104 | 178 | Citizen of the world | Epictetus |
| 105 | 180 | Gratitude to God | Epictetus |
| 106 | 181 | Submission to the Divine will | Epictetus |
| 107 | 182 | Who is the true athlete? | Epictetus |
| 108 | 183 | The free man is the master | Epictetus |
| 109 | 184 | Living according to Nature | Epictetus |
| 110 | 185 | On "attaching yourself to God" | Epictetus |
| 111 | 188 | Gratitude, justice, and steadfastness | The Qu'rân (Koran) |
| 112 | 189 | Remembering God and remembered by Him | The Qur'ân |
| 113 | 191 | The stewardship of God's mercies | The Qur'ân |
| 114 | 193 | Abraham turns from the heavenly bodies | The Qur'ân |
| 115 | 193 | God, the beginning and the end | The Qur'ân |

C. RELIGION IN SOCIETY AND THE STATE

| 116 | 199 | Good government a duty | The Shû King, Chinese (Müller) |

# Index of Subjects and Sources

| SEC. | PAGE. | SUBJECT. |
|---|---|---|
| 117 | 200 | Responsibility of the Ruler |
| | | The Shû King (Müller) |
| 118 | 201 | The sovereign the pattern of excellence . The Shû King (Müller) |
| 119 | 202 | The thoughts should be fixed on learning |
| | | The Li Ki (Müller) |
| 120 | 204 | Virtue independent of circumstance . Plato: The Laws |
| 121 | 206 | The intelligence of the universe is social |
| | | Marcus Aurelius Antoninus: Discourses |
| 122 | 208 | The state and its laws |
| | | Epictetus: The Manual |
| 123 | 211 | The claims of humanity |
| | | From the Roman (Schermerhorn) |

## II. PRAYERS

### A. Collects of Universality

| SEC. | PAGE. | SOURCE. |
|---|---|---|
| 1 | 215 | Liturgy of the Jewish Church |
| 2 | 216 | Alexandrian Liturgy. 175-254 |
| 3 | 218 | Synod of Dort. 1618. Prayer of Balthazar Lydius |
| 4 | 219 | James Martineau. 1805-1899 |
| 5 | 220 | Syrian Clementine. 400. |
| 6 | 220 | Rowland Williams. 1817-1835 |
| 7 | 221 | Gregorian. 7th century |
| 8 | 221 | Mozarabic. Before 700 |
| 9 | 221 | Rowland Williams |
| 10 | 223 | Leonine Sacramentary. 440 |

## Index of Subjects and Sources

| SEC. | PAGE. | SOURCE. |
|---|---|---|
| 11 | 223 | Mozarabic |
| 12 | 224 | Rowland Williams |
| 13 | 224 | Mozarabic |
| 14 | 225 | Liturgy of St. Mark. 171–254 (?) |
| 15 | 225 | Gelasius. 490. |
| 16 | 226 | Rowland Williams |
| 17 | 226 | Rowland Williams |
| 18 | 226 | Book of Common Prayer. 1626 |
| 19 | 226 | Book of Christian Prayers. 1518 |
| 20 | 227 | Rowland Williams |
| 21 | 227 | Thomas à Kempis. 1380–1471 |
| 22 | 228 | James Martineau |
| 23 | 228 | Rowland Williams |
| 24 | 229 | Leonine Sacramentary. 440 |
| 25 | 229 | St. Anselm. 1033–1109 |
| 26 | 229 | Rowland Williams |
| 27 | 230 | Jacobite Liturgy of St. Dionysius |
| 28 | 230 | Rowland Williams |
| 29 | 231 | Ludovius. 1578 |
| 30 | 231 | Eugene Bersier. 1574 |
| 31 | 232 | Rowland Williams |
| 32 | 232 | Sarum Breviary. 1085 |
| 33 | 232 | Liturgy of St. Mark. 175–254 |
| 34 | 233 | Rowland Williams |
| 35 | 233 | Mozarabic |
| 36 | 234 | E. B. Pusey. 1800–1882 |
| 37 | 234 | St. Anselm |
| 38 | 235 | Rowland Williams |
| 39 | 235 | Benjamin Jenks. 1646–1724 |
| 40 | 236 | Greek Church |
| 41 | 237 | Rowland Williams |
| 42 | 237 | Wickes' Devotions. 1700 |

# Index of Subjects and Sources

| SEC. | PAGE. | SOURCE. |
|---|---|---|
| 43 | 238 | Liturgy of St. Mark |
| 44 | 238 | James Martineau |
| 45 | 239 | Rowland Williams |
| 46 | 239 | Treasury of Devotion. 1867 |
| 47 | 240 | E. B. Pusey |
| 48 | 240 | Rowland Williams |
| 49 | 241 | Book of Prayers. 1851 |
| 50 | 241 | Henry Alford. 1810–1871 |
| 51 | 242 | Sarum Breviary. 1085 |
| 52 | 242 | Rowland Williams |
| 53 | 243 | E. B. Pusey |
| 54 | 243 | Coptic Liturgy of St. Cyril. 4th century |
| 55 | 243 | Rowland Williams |
| 56 | 243 | Book of Common Prayer. 1626 |
| 57 | 244 | Rowland Williams |
| 58 | 244 | Rowland Williams |
| 59 | 245 | Rowland Williams |
| 60 | 245 | Sacramentary of St. Gelasius |
| 61 | 246 | Theodore Parker |
| 62 | 249 | Mozarabic |

B. COLLECTS OF ETHICAL AND SPIRITUAL RELIGION

| 63 | 253 | Jewish Liturgy |
|---|---|---|
| 64 | 253 | Jewish Liturgy |
| 65 | 254 | Liturgy of St. James |
| 66 | 255 | Coptic Liturgy of St. Basil. 4th century |
| 67 | 255 | Book of Common Prayer |
| 68 | 256 | Gelasian |
| 69 | 256 | Daybreak office of Eastern Church |
| 70 | 256 | Gelasian |
| 71 | 257 | Book of Common Prayer |

## Index of Subjects and Sources

| SEC. | PAGE. | SOURCE. |
|---|---|---|
| 72 | 257 | Book of Common Prayer |
| 73 | 257 | Midnight office of Eastern Church |
| 74 | 257 | Gallican Sacramentary. 5th century |
| 75 | 258 | Mozarabic |
| 76 | 258 | Book of Common Prayer |
| 77 | 258 | Mozarabic |
| 78 | 259 | Mozarabic |
| 79 | 259 | Gallican Sacramentary. 5th century |
| 80 | 259 | Jeremy Taylor. 1613-1667 |
| 81 | 260 | Thomas à Kempis. 1380-1471 |
| 82 | 261 | Book of Common Prayer |
| 83 | 261 | Sarum Breviary. 11th century |
| 84 | 261 | Christina G Rossetti. 1830-1894 |
| 85 | 261 | William Bright |
| 86 | 262 | Mozarabic |
| 87 | 262 | Book of Common Prayer |
| 88 | 262 | Book of Common Prayer |
| 89 | 262 | St. Theresa. 1515-1583 |
| 90 | 263 | St. Anselm |
| 91 | 263 | Liturgy of St. James. 4th century |
| 92 | 264 | Book of Common Prayer |
| 93 | 264 | Book of Common Prayer |
| 94 | 265 | Mozarabic |
| 95 | 265 | Liturgy of St. Mark. 175-254 (?) |
| 96 | 266 | Henry VIII.'s Primer. 1545 |
| 97 | 266 | Mozarabic |
| 98 | 266 | Roman Breviary |
| 99 | 267 | Coptic Liturgy of St. Basil |
| 100 | 267 | St. Augustine. 354-430 |
| 101 | 268 | St. Augustine |
| 102 | 268 | Book of Common Prayer |
| 103 | 269 | Book of Common Prayer |

# Index of Subjects and Sources

| SEC. | PAGE. | SOURCE. |
|---|---|---|
| 104 | 269 | Mozarabic |
| 105 | 269 | Erasmus. 1467-1536 |
| 106 | 270 | Leonine Sacramentary. 5th century |
| 107 | 270 | Book of Common Prayer |
| 108 | 271 | Book of Common Prayer |
| 109 | 271 | Roman Breviary |
| 110 | 271 | Sarum Breviary. 11th century |
| 111 | 271 | Rowland Williams |
| 112 | 272 | Book of Common Prayer |
| 113 | 272 | Book of Common Prayer |
| 114 | 272 | Roman Breviary |
| 115 | 272 | St. Augustine |
| 116 | 273 | Rowland Williams |
| 117 | 273 | Protab Chunder Mozoomdar. 1840 |
| 118 | 273 | Rowland Williams |
| 119 | 274 | Leonine Sacramentary. 5th century |
| 120 | 274 | Rowland Williams |
| 121 | 274 | Mozarabic |
| 122 | 275 | Rowland Williams |
| 123 | 275 | James Martineau |
| 124 | 275 | Rowland Williams |
| 125 | 276 | Mozarabic. Blessing of the great Paschal Candle on Easter eve |
| 126 | 277 | St. Augustine |
| 127 | 277 | Gelasian. 5th century |
| 128 | 278 | Rowland Williams |
| 129 | 278 | James Martineau |
| 130 | 279 | Rowland Williams |
| 131 | 279 | James Martineau |
| 132 | 279 | Rowland Williams |
| 133 | 279 | James Martineau |
| 134 | 280 | Rowland Williams |

## Index of Subjects and Sources

| SEC. | PAGE. | SOURCE. |
|---|---|---|
| 135 | 281 | James Martineau |
| 136 | 282 | James Martineau |
| 137 | 283 | William Bright |
| 138 | 283 | Sarum Breviary. 11th century |
| 139 | 283 | Roman Breviary |
| 140 | 283 | Roman Breviary |
| 141 | 284 | Greek Church |
| 142 | 284 | George Dawson. 1821 |
| 143 | 285 | James Martineau |
| 144 | 285 | Roman Breviary |
| 145 | 285 | Priests' Prayer Book |
| 146 | 286 | Christina G. Rossetti |
| 147 | 286 | Book of Prayers. 1851 |
| 148 | 286 | Roman Breviary |
| 149 | 287 | Gelasian Sacramentary. 5th century |
| 150 | 287 | Simplicius. 5th century |
| 151 | 288 | Liturgy of St. Chrysostom |
| 152 | 288 | Daybreak office of Eastern Church |
| 153 | 288 | Thomas Aquinas. 13th century. Translated by the Princess Mary |
| 154 | 289 | Book of Common Prayer |
| 155 | 290 | Book of Common Prayer |

C. COLLECTS OF RELIGION—SOCIETY AND THE STATE

| SEC. | PAGE. | SOURCE. |
|---|---|---|
| 156 | 293 | Jewish Liturgy |
| 157 | 293 | Jewish Liturgy |
| 158 | 294 | Book of Common Prayer. Revision of 1883 |
| 159 | 295 | Liturgies of King Edward VI. 16th century |
| 160 | 296 | Liturgies of King Edward VI. |
| 161 | 297 | James Martineau |
| 162 | 298 | James Martineau |
| 163 | 298 | James Martineau |

# Index of Subjects and Sources

### D. Doxologies and Benedictions

| SEC. | PAGE. |
|---|---|
| 164 | 303 |
| 165 | 303 |
| 166 | 303 |

## III. HYMNS

### A. Hymns of Universality

PAGE.
307 One and universal Father
                                  Union (Jewish) Hymnal
308 O Holy Ghost, Thou God of peace
                                  Isaac Williams, 1802–1865
308 Immortal Love, forever full
                                  J. G. Whittier, 1807–1892
309 God of ages and of nations
                                  Samuel Longfellow, 1819–1892
310 Wherever through the ages rise . Whittier
311 City of God, how broad and far
                                  Samuel Johnson, 1822–1882
312 One holy Church of God appears
                                  Samuel Longfellow
313 We believe in Human Kindness
                                  From "Good Words"
314 No human eyes Thy face may see
                                  T. W. Higginson
315 O Life that maketh all things new
                                  Samuel Longfellow
315 O Love Divine, whose constant beam
                                  Whittier
316 O thou not made with hands
                                  F. T. Palgrave, 1824–1900

## Index of Subjects and Sources

PAGE.

317 From heart to heart, from creed to creed
    W. C. Gannett
318 All hail, God's angel, Truth!    W. Newell
319 Eternal Ruler of the ceaseless round
    John W. Chadwick
320 Upon one land alone . . M. J. Savage
321 Out from the heart of nature rolled
    Ralph Waldo Emerson, 1803–1882
322 Life of Ages, richly poured . Samuel Johnson
323 Life of Ages, richly poured . Samuel Johnson

B. HYMNS OF NATURAL, ETHICAL, AND SPIRITUAL RELIGION

327 O worship the King, all-glorious above!
    Sir Robert Grant, 1785–1838
328 Immortal, invisible, God only wise
    W. C. Smith
330 O Father of our spirits   T. W. Chignell
331 God of the earth, the sky, the sea . Anon.
332 I cannot find Thee; still on restless pinion
    Eliza Scudder
333 Go not, my soul, in search of Him
    F. L. Hosmer
335 He hides within the lily . . . Gannett
336 We pray no more, made lowly wise . Hosmer
337 Infinite Spirit, who art round us ever
    James Freeman Clarke, 1810–1888
338 The Lord is in His Holy Place . . Gannett
339 Where is thy God, my soul?
    T. T. Lynch, 1818–1871
340 The King of love my Shepherd is
    Sir Henry Baker, 1821–1877

PAGE.
341  O Love that casts out fear
              Horatio Bonar, 1808–1889
341  Mighty Spirit, gracious Guide
              Bishop Christopher Wordsworth, 1807–1885
343  O Love divine, that stoop'st to share
              O. W. Holmes, 1807–1894
343  Thou hidden love of God, whose height
              G. Tersteegen, 1697–1769
344  Let all men know, that all men move
              Archbishop Trench, 1807–1886
345  At first I prayed for Light
              Mrs. E. D. Cheney
346  Lord of might and Lord of glory
              Union (Jewish) Hymnal
347  Now thank we all our God
              Union (Jewish) Hymnal
347  Early will I seek Thee
              Solomon Ib'n Gabirol, 11th century
              Tr. by G. Gottheil
348  Brief life is here our portion
              Bernard of Cluny, 1091–1153
349  Thou One in all, Thou All in one    S. C. Beach
350  Thou long disowned, reviled, oppressed
              Eliza Scudder
351  O God, in whom we live and move
              Samuel Longfellow
352  I worship Thee, sweet Will of God
              F. W. Faber, 1814–1863
353  Eternal Life, whose love divine
              Emma E. Marean
353  Father, to Thee we look in all our sorrow
              Union (Jewish) Hymnal

## Index of Subjects and Sources

PAGE.
354 Wilt Thou not visit me?
      Jones Very, 1813–1880
355 Gracious Power, the world pervading
      W. J. Fox, 1786–1864
356 Write Thy law upon my heart
      G. Gottheil
356 One Lord there is, all lords above
      W. B. Ranz
357 My God, how wonderful Thou art . Faber
358 Breathe on me, Breath of God
      E. Hatch, 1835–1889
359 Haste not! haste not! do not rest!
      Goethe, 1749–1832
360 Come, Thou Holy Spirit, come
      King Robert II. of France, 971–1031
361 O God of Truth, whose living Word
      Thomas Hughes, 1823
362 O God! whose thoughts are brightest light
      F. W. Faber, 1814–1863
363 Give to the winds thy fears
      Paul Gerhardt, 1607–1676
364 Firm, in the maddening maze of things
      Whittier
365 To Thee we give ourselves to-day
      Adaptation of old ritual song.
      G. Gottheil
365 God of the earnest heart
      Samuel Johnson
366 Oh, sometimes gleams upon our sight
      Whittier
367 We name Thy name, O God
      F. T. Palgrave

| PAGE. | | |
|---|---|---|
| 368 | Walk in the light! so shalt thou know | L. B. Barton |
| 369 | Give forth thine earnest cry | Union (Jewish) Hymnal |
| 369 | O Everlasting Light! | Horatio Bonar, 1808–1889 |
| 370 | Lead, kindly Light | John Henry Newman, 1801–1890 |
| 371 | Father, in Thy mysterious presence kneeling | Whittier |
| 372 | LORD of all being! throned afar | Holmes |
| 373 | What Thou wilt, O Father, give! | Whittier |
| 374 | Thou hidden source of calm repose | Charles Wesley, 1708–1788 |
| 375 | LORD God, by whom all change is wrought | T. H. Gill |
| 376 | Courage, brother! do not stumble | Norman McLeod, 1812–1872 |
| 377 | Thou LORD of Hosts, whose guiding hand | O. B. Frothingham, 1822–1898 |
| 378 | O God, our Help in ages past | James Watts, 1674–1708 |

### C. HYMNS OF RELIGION—SOCIETY AND THE STATE

| | | |
|---|---|---|
| 383 | God of Might, God of Right | Union (Jewish) Ritual |
| 384 | Men, whose boast it is, that ye . . | Lowell |
| 385 | Oh, it is hard to work for God | F. W. Faber |
| 386 | He whom the Master loved has truly spoken | Whittier |

PAGE.
387 Father, let Thy kingdom come
　　　　　　　　　　　　　　　J. P. Hopps
388 O God of love, O King of peace
　　　　　　　　　　　　　　Sir H. W. Baker
389 Once to every man and nation . . Lowell
390 God bless our native land ! Hymns of the Spirit
391 O Beautiful, my Country . . Hosmer
392 My country ! 't is of thee . . S. F. Smith

www.ingramcontent.com/pod-product-compliance
Lightning Source LLC
Chambersburg PA
CBHW051732300426
44115CB00007B/528